WHY
RUSH LIMBAUGH
IS WRONG

WHY RUSH LIMBAUGH IS WRONG

Or:

The Demise of Traditionalism And The Rise of Progressive Sensibility

as perceived by
Michael Rahman

MIGHTY PEN **PUBLISHING** Santa Monica, CA

Why Rush Limbaugh Is Wrong or: The Demise of Traditionalism And The Rise of Progressive Sensibility. Copyright © 1998 by Michael Rahman. All rights reserved. Printed in the United States of America.

Published by:

Mighty Pen Publishing
1223 Wilshire Blvd. #324
Santa Monica, CA 90403
wrliw@earthlink.net
http://home.earthlink.net/~mightypen/

Rahman, Michael
Why Rush Limbaugh Is Wrong or: The Demise of Traditionalism And The Rise of Progressive Sensibility/ by Michael Rahman.
    1. America—politics and government—commentary. I. Title.
    2. Right and left (Political Science).
    3. Rush Limbaugh.
    4. Criminal justice, Administration of.
    5. Progressivism.
ISBN 0-9647470-0-6
Library of Congress Catalog Card Number: 95-77891

THIS BOOK IS DEDICATED TO FRED VANDEN HEEDE.
A great teacher who, aside from bewildering us with his twisting-turning lessons, taught me most everything I know about essay-style writing, for which I am very, very, very
grateful.

CONTENTS

PRELUDE

This is where I thoughtfully relate to you the reader the objective, purpose, or beginnings of my book. This is a tasking duty admittedly, as even I am uncertain how to describe what I've written. On top of the peculiarities of my own creation, there are serious concerns as to the timeliness and tastefulness of the subject.

The subject matter (and what an enormous matter at that) is Rush Limbaugh. I've been reluctant to tell people the title of my book, even though I am proud of the material within. This is because I'm intensely embarrassed to be in any way associated with Rush Limbaugh. I'm embarrassed to be publishing a book that bears his name and that bears his photo. My book was beget of a moment's inspiration (specifically the times Limbaugh blasted a filmmaker and a musician over which I was taken aback), and was forged not of any particular interest in Limbaugh so much as the social/political issues he discusses.

What's more, I began writing this in 1994 when it still seemed somewhat reasonable to give a damn what Rush Limbaugh had to say. But seeing as how it's taken such a ridiculously long time to publish this Godforsaken thing, the timeliness of it is an inescapable issue as public interest in Limbaugh has long since waned. He's yesterday's news, and has been thoroughly exhausted as a subject of conversation or debate. It's best to let the topic wither and wilt like the man's see-saw ratings.

What remains as potent today as at Limbaugh's height of notoriety is the relevance of what he discusses and represents. To watch much of today's popular entertainment one would think America was awash with open-minded freethinkers. In reality, though, conservatism still reigns supreme amongst the majority. The spectrum of this conservatism is as varied as the people themselves, and how much of it is represented by Limbaugh's creed is certainly questionable. However, that at its peak his radio show claimed 20 million listeners suggests his views are in synch with a great many conservatives. More distressing still is the synchronization of his and politician's beliefs (what with Limbaugh being named an honorary member of the 104th Congress).

THAR HE BLOWS!

In confronting the sheer *girth* of all that makes Limbaugh wrong, I had to accept the fact that there *is* no way of addressing all of the infinitesimal idiocies which constitute the man's beliefs. It would serve little purpose to write a book as full of fatuous filler as Limbaugh's own insomnia-curing compositions. And it'd simply be unduly cruel to subject people to a book on his blubberness that was any more drawn out than needed be. (Yes, I know, making fat jokes is pretty mean-spirited—and with a figure like Limbaugh about as easy as shooting fish in a barrel, or, as it were, harpooning a beached whale—but except for a few irresistible barbs I've managed to resist the temptation . . . as best I could anyway.) And it's not like it takes long to accomplish what I've set out to do; fact is a nice little pamphlet would have served just as well to prove Limbaugh wrong, so simple is the task. Or had I the intention, this could have become a thick, queasily thorough chronicle of all the man's erroneous rantings. But wanting to maintain a more intimate tone, I've opted to focus only on those things which most interest me personally. (And quite frankly I didn't want to expose myself to any more of Limbaugh than absolutely necessary; I may be a lot of things, but I'm no masochist.)

Aptly enough, the first time I really took notice of Limbaugh was when he criticized something close to home for me—a filmmaker (the cinema was my major). He could insult the politicians and our society all he wanted; what did I care? I hated politics and society was too confusing to give any serious thought. But when he came on the air and said to millions of people that the only reason Spike Lee made *Malcolm X* was for money, I absolutely couldn't believe it! Was he serious? Had he even *seen* the movie?

The spark for his criticism was when Spike Lee said all black children should skip school to see *Malcolm X*. I'll admit, it wasn't the brightest idea—why not arrange free screenings at the schools so *all* the children can watch it, like Spielberg's done with *Schindler's List*? But I wonder, if it'd been a movie on how utterly noble our founding fathers were (basically a lot of propaganda patriotism) and it was Ron Howard who'd said children should skip school to see his film, would Limbaugh's reaction have been equally cruel? Would he have accused Ron Howard of making some "patriotic" movie purely out of greed, call him a charlatan?

From that point forward it didn't take me long to realize just how incredibly askew Limbaugh's opinions on most social and political matters also were. Often he got me so outraged I felt like yelling at the television, or kicking it in, or writing him a real nasty letter. This book seemed like the next best thing.

A few readers may be wondering what makes me qualified to write such a book: *Who the hell am I?* I'm nobody, I'm just me, Michael Rahman. And my qualifications are not those of formal schooling. I have no Ph.D. in psychology, sociology, or political science. (In fact, before diving into this most of my writing interest was in fiction.) Rather, my qualifications are akin to anyone who has sought satisfaction against the gross grievance of another; to anyone who's desired comeuppance against a verbal bully who cowardly attacks those who are no longer around to defend themselves. Such was the specific genesis of this work.

For though Limbaugh's tirade against filmmaker Spike Lee showed him for an artless boob, and his subsequent social/political observations revealed him as a feckless intellectual, it wasn't until he reached deep down into the muck that I saw just what a callous man he truly is. Even with all this previous exposure, not much prepared me for the moment when Limbaugh's normally inane banter became abrasively cruel.

How else to describe Limbaugh's trashing of a popular musician only days after his death, a man whose only fault was being over-revered by the media as a spokesperson for his generation? And though Limbaugh's ultimate point was that this musician wasn't representative of popular sentiment, the heart of his argument was to call the young man a worthless shred of human debris; he even stooped so low as to attack the way the musician dressed, calling him filthy and rotten, as if chubs is in a position to judge anyone else based on their appearance. (For an elaboration of this incident, see Appendix I.)

¿THESIS?

Alright, now listen up. This is how this *thing* is gonna go down. Think of this book as just one long essay—or a lot of short ones—and this as my (sort of) thesis. Through numerous examples I intend to demonstrate why Limbaugh is wrong. What can be concluded because of this, if indeed anything, is left in each reader's hands.

This is not to say I'll spare the unsuspecting reader my opinion (ill-informed and under-researched as it may be). Really this book's title is, more than anything, meant as a joke. Oh, I believe it. But *so what* if he's wrong? What makes this at all significant are the issues he gives so many wacky opinions of his own on.

I'm honestly not sure if it's possible *to* prove Limbaugh wrong, nor do I see any inherent value or benefit in doing so. It's the issues, stupid. That which follows is nothing more—and not-a-thing less—than a conflict of ideas. But then, what more do we have than ideas and beliefs? That is the very stuff all civilizations are made out of and built around. This subjective battleground opens a much vaster and spectacular arena than any objective conflict ever could. It opens the intellectual, moral, and philosophical doorway to discussing a few of the most pressing concerns facing mankind as the new millennium approaches.

However, before grappling the more pertinent issues, I will attempt to provide a few modest insights into you-know-who's character, to dissect his humdrum hooey and bring some light on to whatever it is that makes a Rush Limbaugh tick. This isn't to suggest I've the ability to fully discern his or anybody's true character—all I can speculate on is that which is broadcast on his shows and printed in his publications. And these are hardly the ideal medium through which to ascertain another's inner workings. But when someone is as outspoken and opinionated as Limbaugh, this certainly makes it easier to get a general impression of these things, however based on dubious media sources they may be.

And now, with no further ado, allow me to present you with why Rush Limbaugh is wrong, and stuff.

I'm vaguely aware that there are some people who are attacking my credibility, and if—I notice that none of them are attacking my credibility on my stance on the substance of the issues—and this, I just take this as a testament to my effectiveness and also an attempt like so many others to hop on my back to sell their stupid, worthless book on the benefit of my name.

Rush Limbaugh, responding to a question regarding the book *The Way Things Aren't* by Steve Rendall (of the media watch group Fairness and Accuracy in Reporting)

THE
'US vs THEM'
SYNDROME

The most beguiling of curiosities is that which makes a personality like Rush Limbaugh so hugely popular to begin with. What exactly is it his devoted fans see in him?

Surely this is a multifaceted thing. The psychological aspects aside (which I'll delve into a little further on), there's the man's sheer wit and charm. For although Limbaugh is completely serious about his convictions, one cannot overlook the diversionary factor of his success. He loves the showmanship of it all, and *can* be genuinely amusing (at times). There's little doubt he wouldn't have as big a following were he not so talented at mixing his commentary/criticism with such often wry humor, were his show not so simultaneously entertaining.

This isn't to say, however, that his fans don't take him seriously. Because my fear is that some take him just a little *too* seriously, and of course Limbaugh doesn't do much to discourage this.

Limbaugh wrote in his *The Way Things Ought to Be* book that he tries to provoke people "into thinking for themselves, and not blindly accepting all they are spoon-fed by the media, myself included." How does he do this? By telling his audience that he'll keep up with the news for them and then, as a bonus, also tell them what to think. Paradox? Not according to Limbaugh: "My little offer to think for people motivates them to do just the opposite: to think for themselves."

Oh, so when he tells his audience (over and over again) that he's *all the truth you'll ever need* and that he'll do their thinking for them, this is just his reverse-psychology way of prompting them to think for themselves? Funny then, because I can't seem to recall Mr. Sigmund ever encouraging his audience to get abortions, do drugs or vote Democratic. *Those* things he takes seriously, but when offering to think for them, *that's* when he's just kidding?

Limbaugh downplays the breadth of his considerable influence (and any and all responsibilities that may come along with it) in a variety of ways. One such tactic is to insist that he's not a part of the mainstream media, that he's some kind of lone alternative, an "equal time" minority barely making an audible squeak above the rash of leftist journalists. And as such a rarefied voice, Limbaugh practically deems himself above critical reproach.

He also has a tendency to contrast himself with the government, shoveling digressions like people can just switch his show off but nobody can turn off the government, and that he doesn't have the power to tax or restrict people's freedoms. In that respect he's correct, his power is pretty meager compared to that of the state. But this doesn't automatically exclude him from taking responsibility for what he says or protect and sanctify him from criticism.

Yet another tactic is to say that critics who rebut his views are insulting the intelligence of his audience. And in so doing Limbaugh attempts to enclose himself in a bubble, a self-contained vacuum, in which none of his fans should take criticism of him seriously because, he seems to suggest, if he's a fool then they're even greater fools for listening to him.

But I hardly believe the majority of Limbaugh's listeners take everything he says in equal measure—I suspect there are a fair number who accept *everything* Rush says without a second (or much of a first) thought; and that there are detractors who, though they agree with little he says, enjoy his show on some perverse level anyway; but I'd like to believe that the majority of Limbaugh's audience take most everything he says with a couple tablespoons of salt. 'Cause while they may agree with many of his points (and not without good reason as much of what the man says *is* grounded in common sense), nonetheless there must also be those in his audience whose bullshit detectors sound off on a fairly regular basis. To those people I'd ask that they allow me to present my case without automatically assuming, as Limbaugh suggests, that I hold them in the same esteem as I do him. For though they may not be as flamboyantly well-spoken as Limbaugh, I'd imagine most of his fans are a good deal more discerning and reasonable in the beliefs they hold. Or at least I'd hope they consider themselves such upon finishing this book.

NO NEW NEWS

Another favorite line of Limbaugh's is that his audience doesn't need the rest of the media as long as they've got him. (After all, who needs a halfway objective source of information when Limbaugh's there to screen life through his own impeccable eyes for them?) Again Limbaugh would most likely demur this as another exaggeration. An intentional *absurdity*. Yet it certainly falls in line with his ongoing assumption that the mainstream media is the sole playground of the radical left. Whenever a journalist or media pundit makes an error in their facts or better judgment, or, for that matter, whenever Limbaugh simply disagrees with their position, according to him it's for absolutely no other reason than that they're a bunch of dewy-eyed liberals.

The mainstream media definitely suffers from some weaknesses, but it's not that they're all "liberals"—it's that they're more interested in headlines and ratings than in what's most perspectively important in our lives (not that this is always the easiest thing to assess itself), and then sometimes they're too demure and diplomatic-like, too hesitant to criticize big business or established institutions.

Limbaugh's own greatest journalistic accomplishment was pointing out how President Clinton was elected on intellectually dishonest campaign promises. What—you mean Bill Clinton lied to get elected? Getouttahere! Like this is something new for a politician? That's pretty much the only way a politician *can* get elected; the majority of the voting public don't *want* politicians to talk about all them complicated fact thingys and issue majiggers. They want comforting assurances. (Does the phrase, "Read my lips: No new taxes . . ." ring a bell?) News would be if a politician were elected based on anything *but* exaggerated campaign promises; now *that'd* be a groundbreaking story!

Clinton was playing the politician, putting on whatever mask he felt he needed to please the voters. I don't hold that against him so much. What I do hold against him is how much he's *stayed* the politician and conformed perfectly into the role of president, whose main duty seems to be as that of the government's ultimate PR man. It's sad it has to be that way, but that's what the public is most interested in: Image, not issues.

Still, Clinton's done a decent job. I believe his winning of the presidential election was, however, greatly responsible for the rise of the Christian Coalition as a political power over the past few years. And with a Democrat in office doing what politicians do best (exaggerate, lie), Limbaugh had the perfect target for his own self-righteous slander. The perfect monster to propel himself off of.

PATRIOTIC PARANOIA

Limbaugh is constantly telling his audience he has more proof of how "we are winning." He seems to find it virtually impossible to make any kind of commentary without comparing and contrasting his righteous ideology against that of an opposing, sinister ideology, whether real or simply in his own mind. Which is most likely the reason he has this tendency to blame anything he dislikes on this disease called "liberalism" in comparison to his anecdote: "conservatism."

He writes that, "The frightening thing about these people [liberals] is their insidious nature. They would present much less of a threat to this society if they would simply be honest and open about their agendas. Instead, they disarm us with such harmless platitudes as "we are in favor of clean air" or "we are against poverty." People should be aware of the extent to which our way of life is under siege by an increasing number of groups with candy-coated causes, but poisonous agendas."

What is the liberal agenda?

• ". . . the Socialist Utopians don't tell you that their agenda to end it merely spreads the misery to include more people."

• ". . . they are all based on the same misguided premise held by the

60's radicals: that Utopia is possible. They think that a centralized government authority can bring us Utopia."

• "Remember this about liberals: They survive and thrive on a fundamental belief that the average American is an idiot—stupid, ignorant, uniformed, unintelligent, incapable of knowing what's good for him, what's good for society, what's right and what's wrong. . . . So they impose affirmative action, quotas, welfare."

The process of this 'US vs THEM' syndrome is as follows. Through sweeping generalizations, Limbaugh defines liberals as a threat to our American freedoms. In so doing Limbaugh establishes his extreme conservatism as the natural counteragent to this extreme liberalism. Limbaugh builds the liberal straw man into a freedom hater; he then tears the straw man down with a few patriotic epithets and proclaims victory for conservatism. 'Them' the enemy, 'us' the hero.

Such 'us against them' scapegoats are nothing new. A Senator named Joseph McCarthy did much the same thing against many innocent Americans, except he accused them not of being liberals, but Communists. And unfortunately McCarthy was in a political position to do great harm to those who were victim to his *patriotic* witch hunt. But the sentiment remains just the same today.

Limbaugh is only too eager to accept the torch of patriotic paranoia: "Now that Communism has collapsed . . . it's time we reidentify today's biggest threat to the American way of life. I'm convinced it's what I call the Socialist Utopians. . . . Theirs is an anti-American credo, which abhors American political and governmental institutions and this nation's capitalistic economy. Their value system is at war with the Judeo-Christian tradition upon which this country was founded. . . ."

As such a fervent 'us against them' freedom crusader, Limbaugh believes partisanship is a *healthy* thing. When Republican Congressman Mit Romney said he wasn't into winning or losing or mudslinging, Rush responded to this by laughing at the idea that the American people are tired of partisanship. In his statement, Congressman Romney said he didn't think any significant change would be made from only one side of the aisle, that he wanted to work with Republicans and Democrats alike more on a common ground. Again Limbaugh laughed at this idea, saying change wasn't going to occur with, "Can't we all just get along?"

"The aggressor in combat makes the rules," he went on to say (Halloween '94). Shortly after Clinton's mid-term State of the Union Address, Rush said, "When I look at a liberal, I see someone who needs to be defeated." Limbaugh truly does look at politics as a WAR, us against them, and as long as *they're winning* everything'll be alright. And—harsh as my deduction might sound—this truly is a sort of *delusional* thinking, needing an enemy (a devil, if you will) to defeat and proclaim victory. He *needs* an evil against his good, something to bounce his beliefs off of—his greatness compared to this terribleness. This is why he's so eager to find the conspiracy where one doesn't exist, to make monsters out of shadows. Why he's so quick to pass judgment. (See Appendix II for some of my thoughts on partisanship politics.)

IMAGE IS NOT CHARACTER

And rather than seeking a full, albeit possibly complicated, truth, Limbaugh seems primarily interested in easy answers and surface appearances. Case in point, his ongoing obsession with "character."

Character was Limbaugh's primary argument against Clinton and for Bush in '92, and again for Dole in '96, and is basically one of his largest philosophies/arguments. And, I mean, don't get me wrong, *of course* a person's character is important, that goes without saying. But character is such an absolute intangible. No matter how much drivel a person lays on you or how much they truly open their heart, someone's character is an almost impossible thing to completely assess, especially someone you've never had the pleasure of meeting in person. (Wise words from someone attempting the deconstruction of Limbaugh's own character, don't you think?)

Limbaugh's argument is that we're supposed to trust these politicians to run our country, and to do so we must trust that their character is good. I take the opposite stance and say a politician's character is inassessable and not a reliable indicator of how they'll perform in office, and that no matter how squeaky clean their image none of them should be trusted to do the right thing. Heck, even children are warned not to trust strangers; why then should adults trust politicians? We should watch their every action like hawks . . . *in office*, that is.

A biography of Bill Clinton called *First in His Class*, by David Maraniss, was said to hint towards the suspicion that the president has cheated on First Lady Hillary for many years. Limbaugh believes the fact that the mainstream media never jumped all over this story is highly indicative of how the leftist press is pandering to the president, how incredibly out of touch the media is with what the American public is interested in, out of touch with what's important.

Apparently Limbaugh doesn't realize that this is another person's private business and should in no way be an issue concerning their professional standing, that it in no way affects or reflects their ability to perform their job. It's perfectly alright if Limbaugh feels strongly against adultery, but still, he shouldn't hold these moral judgments over anybody concerning their professional life. As I understand it, cheating on your wife is not yet against the law (although goodness knows if Rush had it his way, the way he thinks things ought to be, adultery most probably *would* be illegal—the primeval punishment for which I dare not even speculate).

Just because a politician's never had an affair, wraps themselves in the American flag and believes in "family values," this hardly means the public should blindly entrust them to run the country. Such overwhelming faith in one's character, or shall I say *image*, is but a desperate grasping for reassurance; if this is the basis on which Limbaugh wishes to judge politicians, then by all means he's more than welcome to do so. I on the other hand prefer to ignore such irrelevancies and focus on what they do *in office* on an unbiased, case to case basis.

They're politicians; all I'm really interested in is their politics.

IS THERE A DRAFT IN HERE?

One of the largest character faults Limbaugh has always pointed out in President Clinton is how he protested our involvement in Vietnam, and how he didn't go fight for his country when drafted. He calls Clinton a hypocrite for not willing to fight in the Vietnam "Conflict" but being willing to send troops to war as president. But the troops sent to Haiti and Bosnia enlisted into the military of their own free will. They enlisted, they knew the risks; Clinton on the other hand was drafted, he didn't *choose* to enter the military, he was being *forced*.

This is the land of the free—which means being free to have allegiance only in that which one chooses.

A free society means having the right to not *always* be patriotic, to not *have* to risk your life, fight or die for some cause you don't believe in, something you aren't. The fact remains that our government forcing unwilling men to kill and die for this country was a far greater threat to and encroachment of American freedoms than any damn war in Vietnam. If we cannot at least learn that historical lesson in retrospect (as Limbaugh and many conservatives continually refuse to do), then what right do we have to call ourselves freedom fighters?

I am in no way condoning the president's decisions to send troops to Haiti or Bosnia, 'cause I'm still unsure as to their wisdom—but I'm certainly not gonna condemn his decisions based on nothing more than his unwillingness to fight some insane war he was being *drafted* into. It's a pretty simplistic rationale to attack Clinton's character as being a larger factor than whether troops really *should* be sent overseas, no matter who makes the decision to do so or what their supposed "character" is.

SECURITY BLANKETS

Limbaugh was absolutely beside himself that President Clinton would say something as human and honest as "we're doing the best we can." (I forget what Clinton was speaking in regard to, but it can easily be seen as pertaining to all his political efforts.) Upon playing this clip on his show, Limbaugh dumbfoundedly asked, "Can you imagine if Bush said that? 'I'm doing the best I can'?" Actually, uh-huh, and it'd have been a step up from what he *did* do while in office (with the exception of puking on Japan's Prime Minister . . . oh, and let us not forget the Gulf War—having survived countless hours of sensory-assaultive

CNN coverage, I can earnestly say, man, that was one *neato* war! Big fun for the whole family).

Limbaugh just doesn't seem to want to know politicians on a human level—it's as if he wants it in his mind that they're *more* than human, like they have these mysterious superhuman powers by which no wrong can come of their actions.

Put simply, he wants sure things. And I believe *this* is the attraction that keeps his audience listening to him, an attraction common to all mankind. And that is simply something to believe in, to accept as truth; people will put their faith in just about anything to ease their troubles in mind. Limbaugh and his conservatism gives people a sense of order in a world overrun by chaos, he provides a feeling of stability and security to people's anarchic lives.

More than anything, what Limbaugh does is inspire confidence. He allows people to rest assured that, sure, the world's a screwed-up place, but none of it's really *that* bad, and it's certainly not their fault or their responsibility—on the contrary, it's their conservative ideology and religious mythology alone that will set things straight again.

The uncertainty of life is terrifying to most people. Rush Limbaugh subsequently appears to spend most of his time building these walls around himself, trying to convince himself that everything is stable and predictable, that life isn't something he must venture out into and experience on his own but that it's all set in stone. It's like he's afraid to open up and perceive it all for himself absent these distorted filters, to truly experience life. Instead his experience seems largely dedicated to coping with the uncertainty of life, with the fear his own ignorance breeds, et al & etc.

HERE I GO, OFF THE DEEP END

He's accused the Clinton administration of using symbolism to essentially brainwash the public ("symbolism over substance," he'd say), and yet the most profound and intelligent solution Limbaugh can come up with for America's labyrinthine problems is to declare, "We need more God in our lives."

Talk about *symbolism* over substance, "God" is the ultimate symbol. Where, Who, and What is God? How is God going to solve our problems? Limbaugh asks relevant questions, yet the typical answer he gives is that liberals are bad/conservatives good, and that we should have "more God in our lives."

I'm not an atheist (though I often tell people I am just to see the priceless expression on their faces) in the sense that I do believe in our spiritual center; we are more than just carbon-based beings born into this world . . . we are concentrated energy, spirits existing in physical manifestation, love, light—shit, I don't know, the unnamable. Our origin.

I am *very-much-so* an atheist, though, in the sense that I don't believe in the religious God. The religious God is little but a myth, and like most such myths it allows us humans to do something we have an inexplicable need to: surrender our free will, hand the reins over to this omnipotent being who wishes us to live only *one* way which is *His* way. Everything describing and relating how God looks, communicates, and rules is completely human, totally lodged in the physical. Heaven is in our sky, in the clouds. That's where God, a white male, lives and looks down upon us. When we die, if we've done His will (which can be found only in the Bible and through holy men), then we become angels in His Kingdom with our wings, flowing white gowns, and of course our halos.

It's a nice picture, isn't it? Simple, easy, requiring no personal awareness or knowledge. *Completely and absolutely symbolic.*

And hell below us, that toasty place in which people burn for all eternity if they've sinned, broken the rules within the Bible. Sort of like the idea of sending people who break the law to a hell-like prison. The whole idea is to instill respect through fear; who cares if you understand the law (God's or society's) or are actually obeying it of your own free will. Simply surrender your will to the omnipotent one and everything will be taken care of, no more worries about having to think and decide for yourself.

Religion allows people to surrender to their inborn lack of inner-guidance. Almost naturally people are inclined to find something outside themselves to compensate for this inner weakness. Thus was born myth and religion, something to give people a sense of objective outward truth—a compensatory sanity to use in substitution for knowledge of their own individual self-will, that which so many have such a difficult time coming to grips with. The abyss in all our minds. That which *is* our fear of the unknown.

I'm not gonna deny the possibility of an afterlife or of a greater power that is the source of this and all existence. But the fact is we know only what we perceive from our physical plane, which is so little. It's time we accepted any possible before-or-afterlife as the great unknown it largely is.

EPILOGUE

I sincerely don't mean to insult anyone's religion, and I am empathetic to the need people feel for a sense of higher order. But neither can I so fear insulting people's religious beliefs that I don't express what I honestly believe to be true. That would be a travesty in and of itself, in the name of the truth, and all that good stuff. (Besides, it'll be helpful to have an idea of my position on religion before directly confronting Limbaugh's approach to the issue.)

SORRY, BUT, NO, RELIGION AND GOVERN-MENT *DO NOT* BELONG TOGETHER!!

Yes, no doubt about it, I am a hard-core proponent of secularism. But don't misinterpret my conviction. I'll defend to the death Rush Limbaugh and everyone's right to practice whatever religion they please. I will not, however, stand back and watch as they forcibly try to subject everyone else to their faith. Particularly young impressionable minds "full of mush," as Limbaugh condescendingly describes today's youth.

Defending classroom prayer, Limbaugh argues: "In no way does the state's allowance of a time period to enable children to commune with their Creator, whoever they deem Him to be or however they choose to communicate with Him, indicate a state preference for a certain denomination." But even Limbaugh's argument is a contradiction onto itself in that it presumes everyone belongs to a faith, and that everyone's religion subscribes to a *male* Creator.

Worst of all is the statement *however they choose to communicate with Him*, something Limbaugh could in no way actually defend. Clearly his definition of "prayer" is as it pertains almost exclusively to Christianity, for what if one's way of *communicating* with their Creator involved screaming profanities at the top of their lungs whilst dripping hot candle wax on their nipples? Sounds absurd, sure, but no more so than many real religions and cults. Would Limbaugh then defend this practice in classrooms? For as he so perceptively put it: ". . . to deny children the time to pray comes closer to violating their exercise of religion than the allowance of that time violates the establishment clause." In other words, it's prayer time children: break out the candle wax and start screaming profanities—it's your constitutional right.

For if Christians start worshipping in class, then the Muslims, Jews, Hari Krisnas and the Satan worshippers should have the same right. So some kids will be praising the Lord; others will be burning incense and chanting; while others will be decapitating chickens and drawing blood pentagrams in honor of the Lord of Flies—basically it'll be a mess. Limbaugh understands this rubs some the wrong way: "People who want to pray to Allah or Buddha will be offended, even if the prayer is nondenominational." Nondenominational? What the fudge! Can there be a greater oxymoron than *nondenominational prayer?* The fact of the matter is that classroom prayer, wholesome as it may be in theory, is almost solely accommodating to the Christian faith, and thus if allowed would be an infringement on other's religious (or non-religious) beliefs.

If you want your kids to pray in their classroom, then send them to a private, religious school.

Obviously kids *should* be allowed to pray in public school. And there are plenty of times they may do so outside their classes. Any time of the day a student can say a private prayer without even drawing attention to the fact. But for those who find comfort in unified prayer, then why not start a Prayer Club like all the other extra-curriculum activities? They could meet and do their prayer thing during lunch, or before or after school. There's absolutely no reason it should be done in a classroom in front of everyone else. Those who think it should be are presumptuous that everyone's in tune with their faith and that their faith is right for everyone.

When the Supreme Court ordered that the Ten Commandments be removed from high school bulletin boards, Limbaugh sarcastically chimed that, yeah, "the Ten Commandments include admonitions such as: Thou shalt not kill, Thou shalt not steal, Thou shalt not covet thy neighbor's wife. Really harmful stuff to expose to young skulls full of mush." The thing is, there are probably hundreds of other religious ideologies that contain similarly moral messages. Are schools supposed to post manuscripts of all those different religious doctrines just because some positive message or lesson is meant to be gleaned from its text? Must they force all faiths onto these kids?

Hey, I have no problem if schools want to teach that stealing and killing are wrong, just so long as the words they use are their own and they don't simply stand there like cavemen, grunting and pointing at the Ten Commandments. And if you feel schools must discourage kids from committing adultery, then your argument for the importance—the necessity—of this lesson had better be your own and not simply because it says so in the Bible.

Limbaugh proclaims: "It's time we . . . returned religion to its honored place in the life of this nation." Much like his loose use of the term "prayer" in the classroom (*nondenominational prayer* at that!), Rush is very non-specific in his use of the word religion. *Whose* religion—*what* religion—is he referring to? All religions? I doubt it. No, he means *his* religion. The *Christian* religion. It is this to which he refers, and nothing more. He says our public school's failure to teach kids the fundamentals of his Christian religion (the Ten Commandments) is nothing less than "depriving children of their moral and mental nutrients during their formative years." He then has the audacity to say he knows the arguments about separation of church and state; it would appear then he just doesn't happen to *agree* with them.

IN GOD I DOUBT

In explaining how necessary religion is to government, Limbaugh gives many excellent examples of just how hypocritical our nation's *separation of church and state* philosophy is; whose side is he trying to prove, anyway? He's eluded to the fact that our government has used religious terminology from its beginning, from monuments and anthems (one nation, under God), the 'In God We Trust' on every currency denomination, to courts of law.

I don't suppose this bothers the average God fearin' citizen who accepts this stuff as easily as the obvious existence of the sun and the moon. But if in all those places where the fuzzy euphemism of God is mentioned in our government, what if they said something more specific like, say, 'Jesus Christ' instead? (That's basically the same thing, is it not?) Then might people begin to understand how grave an encroachment this is on the spiritual freedoms of others, those who do not accept such as their own belief system?

But according to Limbaugh, advocates of secularism are only out to severe America's religious roots. "Those who would undermine America . . . know they have to first chip away at the faith of Americans, at their spiritual foundations." He wrote in *The Way Things Ought to Be* how America was founded flat-out as a Judeo-Christian country; not as a country with tolerance for all faiths, but as specifically a *Christian* country. He explains: "When you look at the documents written by the men who founded this country, you find they were devoted to their [Christian] God."

So these men had passionate religious convictions before there even existed a state to tout its trust in God? Why then is Limbaugh so convinced secularism is prompting "this country to be a Godless one"? Is he suggesting that without this pat reinforcement people would abandon their religious beliefs? He must not have much faith in the faith of others if he deems this the case.

I'd suggest that if Limbaugh truly believes this active government encouragement is so crucial to the spiritual foundation of his Judeo-Christian church-state, then it is *he* who views people in the condescending light he accuses liberals of. I'm not claiming to know the mind of Limbaugh, but there's little denying this stance of his implies a belief that the religious faith of Americans is so weak it must depend on this government reinforcement to sustain itself. And of course if the state doesn't see to it that this Christian faith is sustained, people will naturally look for less holy institutions by which to guide themselves . . . like, say, the very government Limbaugh wants encouraging this religious faith in them to begin with!

R.L.: "If [man's] faith in God is destroyed, the void will be filled with something else. Throughout history that substitute for faith has been a belief in a man-made god called the state. Untold crimes have been committed in its name. . . ." What? And no blood has been spilt in the name of that man-made god called God? Some of the bloodiest and most despicable acts of hate have been waged in the various names of God. Is my point then that faith in God is a dangerous thing to be avoided? No, not at all. I only wish to point out that Limbaugh's one-sided criticism of the state is in no way a valid example by which to contrast the holiness of faith. And it's certainly no basis on which to argue for our government's establishment of a Supreme Being.

Because, contrary to what Limbaugh says, the First Amendment *is* more than just Freedom of Religion; it *is* also Freedom *from* Religion. The freedom to pursue our own individual spirituality without being bombarded and subject to other people's religious dogmas.

Unfortunately some are so emotionally dependent on their faith, and so convinced that they're right, *only they're right*, they tend to believe that the planet will fall apart into unmitigated chaos unless ruled by their mythology. Those in the grips of such religious fanaticism need to question whether they truly appreciate or understand the principles of freedom on which America was founded.

SCHOOL'S FOR TEACHING, CHURCH IS FOR PREACHING

Limbaugh suggests the decline of America's education system corresponds to when the government made it more religiously neutral, quoting Supreme Court Judge Clarence Thomas: "My mother says that when they took God out of the schools, the schools went to hell." Our schools are obviously in weak shape, but can they really be seen as a decline compared to when Christianity still loomed large in the classrooms? How good could the actual *education* have been back then that it's such a shambles compared to what it is today?

In our nation's infancy an education, even literacy, were considered luxuries of the privileged and upper-class. I mean, what kind of strong emphasis has our country *ever* put on the importance of an education?

A teacher is one of the highest paid and respected professions there is in many Asian nations. This must be because they value knowledge and wisdom as some of the greatest things in life—unlike other countries I can think of. Teachers here are held up as not much more than underpaid civil servants. Our government reveres the teachers it hires about as much as its bureaucratic paper-pushers. Being a public school teacher is one of the least paid, undervalued professions there is in our country. We seriously do seem to care more about smart bombs than smart kids; the logic seemingly being who needs an educated offspring when we have the power to just *kill* everything?

To put this in a broader perspective, one must also take into account how the last hundred years has seen an increase in our knowledge that is utterly unprecedented. Not to deny that many important discoveries have been made all throughout human history, but still, on a graph our thousands of years of previous history would be a fairly stagnant line compared to the sharp spike of growth that's occurred recently. Ours has been a slowly evolving awareness, till suddenly with the boom of industry and technology (for better or for worse) we've skyrocketed as a people, literally to the moon and beyond.

So really the education today is better simply by virtue of the fact that we *know* so much more now. I imagine then the major difference Limbaugh's referring to when he speaks of the "decline" of our education system is the behavior of the students. And while kids of eras past might indeed have been better behaved, that's hardly reflective of the *quality* of the education they we're receiving, simply that they were easier to keep in line (which shouldn't be surprising—the less educated people are, naturally the easier they are to control).

But today's youngsters are not so afraid to express what they think; to ask questions to which those in authority currently have no answers. And for the last half century, each new generation has reached a level of mental maturity far greater than the previous, with a longing for a more open and honest education than their teachers can deal with, having come from a painfully different time themselves.

This gap is not only generational, but also institutional. For though religion may have been removed from the classrooms, its authoritarian attitude lingered. And as far as the school system has progressed since those days, it still adheres to fairly simplistic "deference to authority" teaching practices. (So it shouldn't be in the least surprising that modern kids are rebellious—nor should this necessarily be seen as something bad. It just means they're eager to progress past the tired norms of a stalemate culture.)

Not only has the school system failed to make any great strides, but there are many who believe it's gone way too far already, such as with its approach to sex education.

PURITANS NO LONGER

There's nothing wrong with telling kids straight-up that the only sure-fire way to protect themselves against sexually transmitted diseases and from becoming pregnant is through abstinence. But there is something *extremely* wrong if this is the centerpiece of a sex education curriculum. Encouraging kids to abstain of their own free will is one thing, but to teach them *nothing* but abstinence is downright dangerous. If taught that the only safe sex is no sex, how can they possibly be expected to protect themselves if they *do* decide to, uh, bump uglies?

Teachers can encourage abstinence *and* teach about birth control in the same class. Not according to Limbaugh, though—to him (like most things) it's a simplistic black and white, one or the other situation. Either you're teaching kids right from wrong—abstinence—or you're "teaching that sex does not have any consequences," which he believes "is the selfish agenda these people hold dear."

Limbaugh also contends that condoms promote *free love*, àla Austin Powers (*yeah baby*). He says, "Condom distribution sanctions, even encourages, sexual activity, which in teen years tends to be promiscuous [he only wishes he spoke from experience] and relegates to secondary status the most important lesson to be taught: abstinence."

But just because schools make condoms available, or even distribute condoms to students, how is this going to encourage them to do something that they otherwise wouldn't? Cripes, most guys have a hard enough time getting laid as is, but Limbaugh's gonna have us believe just because they've got a condom all these girls are gonna go, "Oh, okay," and throw their legs open? Puh-leeze!

Limbaugh defines his own term *Young Skulls Full of Mush* as: "Young American people after their brains have been pasteurized and filled with multiculturalism, sex advocacy programs, and other twaddle by our failing public school system." But Limbaugh reveals his own supercilious condescension by portraying kids as deciding to have sex with the rationale of simpletons: "Heck, the *school gave me this condom*, they know what they're doing." Apparently Limbaugh doesn't believe teenagers are at risk of having their minds *turned* to mush quite so much as he believes that they're inherently at risk because their minds are *already* mush.

Schools probably shouldn't distribute condoms to all students whether they asked for them or not, I think that's a bit personal. Rather, they should simply make condoms easily available to those who want them. But by no means do I buy into this myth that by handing a student a condom we've encouraged them to have sex; kids aren't as dumb as Rush would have us believe. Kids can recognize birth control as something they might use *if* they choose to have sex, but this knowledge certainly isn't going to influence that most personal and emotional decision.

And if they don't have any protection, does Limbaugh believe this is going to stop a couple from having sex if that's their intention? It might delay it for a couple hours, days or weeks, but sooner or later they'll find a contraceptive. Either that or they'll go ahead and have sex without any protection at all, and that's just a simple unstoppable fact, whether people want to accept it or not.

Limbaugh takes the "kids are going to do it anyway, you can't stop them" notion to its logical conclusion by arguing that, hey, if we're gonna give kids condoms, why stop there? Why not convert study hall into Safe Sex Centers where students can have sex in school, why not put disease-free hookers in these Safe Sex Centers? As Limbaugh puts it: ". . . if safe sex is the objective, why compromise our standards?" Hey, if abstinence is his objective, why not carry *that* to its logical conclusion and castrate the boys and sew up the girls? Why compromise your standards, right Rush?

Today's sex ed is so highly improved compared to that of half a century ago, a time of prudery and repression to which Limbaugh implies we should return. You watch those old b&w health education films of the 40's and 50's and on the surface they're just laughably hokey, but listen to their exact content and you'll notice they were extremely conforming. They had nothing to do with the actual changes that take place during puberty. Instead they were almost solely a particular group or person's personal beliefs being objectified into this presentation of what was "normal, acceptable behavior," as if there *were* such a clearly discernible thing.

Kids are obviously having sex these days at younger and younger ages, but their behavior is influenced more by society than their school, having to do with these radical advancements in technology and how this has shaped our pop-culture. (And you want to know something? People have *always* had sex at ages or under circumstances others considered inappropriate, so at least in that respect things remain unchanged.)

Besides, if people can't deal with their kids growing up and becoming sexually intimate, then the real problem is their poor parenting and desire to have the schools and society raise their children for them.

CONCLUSION

There are, to be sure, a lot of lousy, half-ass parents out there resulting in some pretty screwy kids. But all the schools can do is give students the most thorough and honest education possible, and simply hope they'll use that knowledge to make their own best decisions. It's not, nor should it be, the school's responsibility to preach the puritanical values of this country's religious majority.

Limbaugh says: "The way to improve our schools is not more money, but the reintroduction of moral and spiritual values, as well as the four "R's": reading, 'riting, 'rithmatic, and Rush."

Other than increasing teachers salaries (which is the only way they'll attract better quality teachers to public schools), I agree that schools don't need more money—what's needed is better *management* of its funds. They need to really show where the priorities are; that is, in the classrooms, not the operation of the bureaucratic school administrations. What I *disagree* with Rush about is the need for the preaching and prayer of the Christian religion (see Appendix III), or as he put it, "... the reintroduction of moral and spiritual values...." What schools really need is more creative classroom environments where students feel like a real part of the process of their own education; where they're talked with and not at; where they are able to freely express and develop their own voices. The entire curriculum of the school should reflect such nurturing tendencies.

ON THE
LIGHTER SIDE

SWEET TOOTH SACRILEGE

No one would want to deny another person the little things in life that somehow make the whole great mess almost bearable. Such as the pleasure of eating delicious food, a sensory stimulation that's comparable to drug addiction the way some people overindulge. Certainly junk food can be consumed safely in moderation; but how are people supposed to know to eat it in moderation unless they know it's *junk?* Limbaugh, however, takes the attitude that anyone who tells people that something's unhealthy is also telling them that they should *never* eat it, how to live their lives; this may be what his mind hears, but it's *not* what's being said.

Such was his reaction when the Center for Science in the Public Interest (CSPI) released data stating that popcorn cooked in coconut oil is high in cholesterol. The author of the study, one Jayne Hurley, said of it, "Popcorn is only as good as what you cook it in." Now is that the rantings of someone telling people how to live their lives, that they should never touch popcorn again?

But according to Limbaugh, CSPI is just a bunch of ninny-ninny worry warts with nothing better to do than ruin everyone's happiness. So-stinking-what if they disclosed this popcorn's cholesterol content? Doesn't the public have a right to be informed? If some guy's suffering from heart disease, shouldn't he be made aware that this popcorn is high in cholesterol?

Limbaugh says the media is "constantly pounding us with doom and gloom scenarios, which often cast a negative spell over the national psyche." But in truth it seems Limbaugh would prefer to simply stick his head in the sand than face any kind of unpleasant reality. He acts like he'd rather just live in darkness of this knowledge because now he has to think and care about it. (Reminds me of a *Seinfeld* episode where Jerry and Elaine unveiled that the supposedly nonfat frozen yogurt was actually loaded with fat, and the Newman character resented it because, even though it was bad for him, he would have preferred not to know and continue eating it like there was no tomorrow.) And heaven forbid Rush should have to think twice before stuffing his face with all his favorite goodies.

It's because of my intentionally limited exposure to Limbaugh that I'm unable to give more detailed examples of all the absurd hysterics he's gone into over health information that's made it into the news. But the one time I saw him do this "Scare of the Week" segment on his television show, Limbaugh accused some group (who were championing cooking methods that reduce exposure to the *E. coli* bacteria) of being more scare mongers trying to create a panic. Yeah, tell that to the parents of those children who died after eating undercooked burgers at Jack in the Crack.

What's particularly unusual about this is that Limbaugh's constantly claiming how he's all about encouraging his audience to think for themselves—and punctuates this point by accusing the "mainstream" media of looking upon his audience as a lot of sheep. But how is Limbaugh looking upon his audience when he says this health stuff is just the work of people trying to ruin their happiness, saying it's meant to frighten them? By treating his audience as though they're incapable of dealing with such information without it creating this irrational fear?

He claims "liberal" news reporters and politicians underestimate the intelligence of the American public—yet how much credit is Limbaugh giving anyone when he reacts to this health and nutrition stuff like he does? The fact remains that only an ignorant person *would* be scared or put into a panic by such information.

SECONDHAND STUPEFACTION

Not only is Limbaugh convinced public interest groups like CSPI are backhandedly out to smear the good name of junk food, he furthermore disputes those who would have us believe that secondhand smoke is dangerous. To prove such he cited a scientific study which concluded that certain everyday vegetables have as much nicotine in them as spending three hours in a smoke-filled room. And no one's ever died from eating vegetables, have they?

Heh, really, this is absurd enough as to be outright comical.

It just might have occurred to a smoker such as Limbaugh that tobacco nicotine goes into the lungs (that's why it's called *lung* cancer!) and the nicotine in vegetables never does. It goes directly into the stomach—and is digested by stomach acids and distributed throughout the body. That's because, unlike tobacco, vegetables are a food. The act of eating is a little different than that of breathing. And so to compare the harmful effects of inhaling cigarette smoke and grubbing on some vegetables makes zero sense. Which just about makes it the epitome of Limbaugh's prodigious wisdom.

Furthermore, to claim that secondhand smoke is harmless is the equivalent of saying smoking is itself harmless. It's simply not possible that cigarette smoke could be harmful to smokers but not others; likewise, if the smoke isn't bad for secondhand inhalers, then it must also be harmless to smokers. And who in good conscious could claim such a thing? Other, of course, than the tobacco industry itself, but they've got profit margins to look out for and can't be bothered with petty things like a conscious. I swear, when the heads of the tobacco companies told that Congressional Health Committee they don't believe there's any evidence to show that smoking is addictive or dangerous, it made me want to puke all over their nicotine-stained suits! If people want to slowly smoke themselves to death, then by all means they should have every right to do so. But as long as the tobacco industry denies that their cigarettes are harmful when they consciously know otherwise, then each person that dies and all the millions of deaths that have already occurred due to smoking related causes can't be considered slow suicides, but rather homicides. And as such the tobacco companies should be held responsible for these deaths—not criminally, but most definitely financially.

Also of questionable conscious is Limbaugh, who likewise says: "There is no conclusive proof that nicotine's addictive . . . and the same thing with cigarettes causing emphysema, lung cancer, heart disease." You'd think even—and especially—the most ardent of smokers would recognize the malfeasance of the companies getting rich off their addictions. To assert that secondhand smoke is harmless because of some vegetables with nicotine in them strikes me as the reasoning of a person deeply in denial, not unlike the tobacco companies themselves. Except it's reasonable to assume that these companies are privy to the dangers of smoking but deny this to protect their profits; whereas with a figure like Limbaugh, it's much harder to get a handle on his motivation for such a denial.

Does Limbaugh genuinely believe smoking to be harmless? Is it denial of the health risks his own smoking puts him at—sheer scientific ignorance—or is he looking out for the profits of tobacco companies? Or rather, could it be nothing more than his desire to smoke in restaurants that he rebuts such dangers?

Given his penchant for cigars and attacking anti-smoking crusaders like Henry Waxman, the latter seems just as likely an explanation. When Limbaugh wants to smoke a cigar after a particularly satisfying meal (which I'm sure is all of them), he certainly doesn't want to have to wobble his settling load outside just to appease a bunch of ninny-ninny liberals, never mind the health of the waitresses and bartenders inhaling smoke eight hours a day. The fact is nicotine is a drug, an exceedingly addictive and deadly one, and there's no reason why employees in a public workplace should have to be the secondhand recipients of this nasty drug.

When he's not busy misinterpreting scientific studies to his own twisted ends, Limbaugh enjoys flying off the handle in regard to any senseless little thing. Once during an eclipse of the sun he mentioned how annoyed he was by all the "eclipse hysteria." What hysteria? There was mild interest at best, what's so wrong with that? It's a grand cosmic event. Okay, so he doesn't think it's a big deal—so friggin' what?! Why not just leave it at that? Because he's incapable of appreciating *anything* outside his way of thinking; and he will criticize anything that doesn't fit into the itty-bitty box of limited perspective he calls his mind.

On top of everything else, Limbaugh also considers himself an expert on the art and business of filmmaking. (As his *Malcolm X* condemnation so clearly demonstrated.) He points out that whenever a Disney cartoon is released it slaughters everything else in the marketplace, and they're are all 'G' rated. And so he doesn't understand why these idiot filmmakers aren't all making 'G' rated family pictures, 'cause, he says, they're obviously the films making the most money. But of the 50 top-grossing films of all time, only four are 'G' rated. The fact is nowadays a 'G' rating is practically the kiss of box office death. Disney cartoons kick ass at the box office not *because* they're rated 'G,' but because they're *Disney*.

I'm still uncertain as to why Limbaugh considers Oliver Stone an "anti-American" filmmaker. How could anyone imply that *Platoon* is anything other than an honorable tribute to the men who fought and died in that horrendous war? How exactly is *Wall Street* anti-American? It's not against the capitalist free market, it's simply an examination of extreme greed, the blind lust and worship of money.

Though I remember Limbaugh once said that money was the only thing that actually motivates anyone to do anything. Money and nothing else is why anyone ever does anything—he actually said this, oh yes. The reason I'm writing this book right now is for the exact same reason someone works on Wall Street—just trying to get rich as I can. Because that's all anyone *really* cares about. Right? And that's the only truly measurable yardstick of success: ultimate wealth and power. Right Rush? (But enough with this light stuff.)

MORE INEVITABLE
THAN TAXES

OR:

AND NOW ON THE DARKER SIDE

Life can be described in many ways and from an infinite variety of vantage points. But in my estimation it can be most simply perceived as a journey of ever-broadening knowledge and experience, a trip in which one travels from no understanding to all understanding. And death being one of the most traumatic and yet essential occurrences of our lives, it seems to me that a people's attitude toward life can (to a certain degree) be gauged by the attitude they take toward death. No, I'm not just prattling on like this to demonstrate how thoughtful I am, I actually am leading to something. . . .

And that is that, when it comes to dying, little is more controversial than the medical practice by which the process is sped up. Specifically I mean euthanasia, *not* mercy killings. And sensible, professional euthanasia, not just helping someone to commit suicide in the back of a van while driving them to the morgue. That said, though, I'm gonna talk about Jack Kevorkian anyway.

When Dr. Kevorkian was found not guilty of murder for an assisted suicide in Michigan, Limbaugh played videotape of some of the jurors explaining how they had reached their verdict. One particular juror said his decision was based on the facts of the case, but then went on to say how maybe it was also influenced by his own life experience. He was announced clinically dead in 1973, and of this he nonchalantly said, "And I guess it wasn't that bad."

Needless to say Limbaugh couldn't *believe* this (it was a strange statement to be sure—I thought harmless and amusing). But Limbaugh then said he doesn't believe movie or television violence is responsible for all the violence in our society, but they're the only reason he can fathom somebody dying and actually saying it wasn't that bad. By this it sounded as though he is quite terrified of dying, not unlike most humans. I've always found it odd how those who so faithfully embrace this cloudy vision of "heaven" are also so terrified of their own mortality. (Perhaps because the Bible describes such a conditional and vengeful God.)

Of course life is better than death for those in their prime, but when already slipping swiftly down that slope, painfully so, then how can embracing one's ultimate fate be a bad thing? But Limbaugh, like many, can't seem to equate death with anything but the ultimate shaft.

Limbaugh scoffs at the notion that euthanasia benefits the patient who wants it because, though they may be in terrible pain, it's simply a matter of taking into account the alternative: Death. Course it's rather easy for him to say it won't benefit the patient when *he's* not the one suffering; yet still, were he in the most horrific pain imaginable he'd probably still reject the notion of euthanasia, for his fear is so great that I don't believe even miserably teetering on the unstoppable brink will he ever accept the inevitability of his own death. (And thus till his last breath will he scorn those who *do* accept their own deaths, fight to deny them the personal right of euthanasia, and will continue to preach how liberals are undermining all respect for human life.)

DEATH IS OUR SOCIETIES GREATEST FEAR

Well, actually, death isn't quite people's *greatest* fear. It's second only to public speaking. Having taken a speech class I can verify that—it was a terrifying experience alright. But a fun fear to face. Most people never think to overcome a fear like that, much like they never question their fear of death. Now I'm not talking about the rational fear everyone possesses of being prematurely killed, but there is a pretty radical difference between possessing a healthy instinct for survival and a conditioned fear of the unknown. People are so afraid of their own physical mortality that they've turned death into the big bad bogeyman lurking under the bed or hiding in the closet, and these fearful souls are going to oppose it in all its forms, even a dying person's own will to die.

Many opponents make the argument that sometimes when a fatally-ill person is given two years to live, it may turn out to be ten. But do they honestly believe that anyone would want to kill themselves just because they've been told they only have a few years to live? If they weren't suffering, then surely they'd want to live out every last second of that time left. Anyone who wanted to die before they even began feeling the ravages of their disease would clearly be someone in need of therapy, not euthanasia.

Still others reason that if those who want euthanasia die today when they could have conceivably lived a few more days, weeks, or months, then they might have written a poem the likes of which has never before been heard, or they might have done some other precious, significant thing in that time of their greatest suffering. Of course, the same could be said of anyone who dies a natural death . . . if they'd only lived a little longer they might have done this, they *might* have done that. This is called denial folks: trying to find any excuse for why a person should suffer through their pain, prolong their life, and, most importantly, avoid their death for as long as possible. I mean, just imagine all the nifty poems people could write if they *never* died—just imagine all the *might have* possibilities then.

Death is as natural a part of life as anything. It's about time people understood this. And rather than resist all attempts to confront death, people must be willing to accept and, in some cases, even welcome it.

Rush Limbaugh can't imagine accepting death without this causing people to value life less. But by embracing death you are also embracing life. Those afraid to die are almost inevitably afraid to live. There is incredible freedom in being able to transcend one's fear of death—I can hardly imagine a more liberating feeling . . . except, perhaps, for death itself, whatever that is exactly.

Suppose we'll all find out eventually, though for now my curiosity is largely at bay, lest life should pass me by in the meantime. Know what I'm sayin'?

CORRUPTION AND ABUSE

Unsurprisingly, Limbaugh depicts proponents of euthanasia as being more morally bankrupt radicals. "They're not calling for a right to die, they're mostly talking about a right to kill. The advocates of euthanasia are asking the government and courts to step aside and allow people who are feeble and elderly to be snuffed out." Again Limbaugh uses an entirely inaccurate broadstroke to simplify the issue into an expedient duel between himself and devilish liberals.

The most logical argument made is that euthanasia would turn doctors whose job it is to heal into killers. Limbaugh argues that we "shouldn't corrupt the medical profession in this country by allowing "assisted" suicide. . . . When you corrupt the medical profession, you might as well throw away the Hippocratic Oath. Its most basic tenet is: Do No Harm—and that means no harm to human life." He seems to suggest that once this line is crossed, then the floodgates of evil will open and doctors will automatically start abusing all their regular patients or something. I don't know what kind of untrustworthy, portentous physician Rush has been going to, but for any certified and sane doctor it should be pretty easy to separate euthanasia from the rest of their practice.

Besides, I honestly don't feel doctor-assisted suicide *can* be seen as doing harm, not when it's what the patient themselves want. Shouldn't a doctor's main concern be the best interest of each individual patient? Well then, if it's perceived that euthanasia truly is the will of a patient, and if circumstances allow, how can acting according to that patient's wishes be seen as doing harm?

And how exactly would this turn physicians into executioners? We're not talking about doctors just indiscriminately prescribing fatal doses of barbiturates to anyone who hints they may wish to end their suffering.

What we *are* talking about is a steady, professional process of a patient bringing up their feelings of wanting to die without immediately being carted off to the loony bin. And so as to best avoid any possible abuse (as has been suggested by the Hemlock Society), all candidates should have to be evaluated by two independent physicians to determine that their condition is indeed critical. And to a certain degree, I'd imagine, also to make sure the candidate is mentally competent. But Limbaugh argues that anyone who wants to die *can't* possibly be of their right mind. After all, they want to die. And when someone is not only dying but also so crazy from the pain that they actually *want* to die—well now, it'd just be cruel to help such a person kill themselves. That's Limbaugh logic for you.

Actually, the best safeguard is to relax the rules restricting medical use of morphine to ease the suffering of those dying. Once someone is dying and in great pain, then I say give them all the drugs they want. Let their final days not be ones of agony.

Also important to preventing abuse is to make sure that the dying get the best care possible such as being in Hospices as opposed to hospitals, and improving their life to the best of those circumstances.

But if all that were done and someone, because of great pain, still wills to end their own life, then that person should also have the choice of doing so with dignity. To knowingly say their final good-byes to family and loved ones; and to do nothing more criminal than end their own suffering and embrace what they know to be every mortal being's inevitable and ultimate conclusion.

THE UNWINNABLE WAR

America spends hundreds of billions of dollars on its "War on Drugs" (a major sum of which is generated by grossly unjust mandatory minimum sentencing laws), and no, don't be misled by those exciting busts on *Cops*, we're nowhere near winning the war. Drugs are more readily available than ever. They are rampant throughout the entire country.

And while indeed most illegal drugs *are* dangerous and *can* destroy people's lives (not to mention lead people to lives of crime to support their addiction), the fact is the selling and using of drugs by itself isn't a violent crime. It is passive, and harms no one directly except for those who choose to use.

To wage a multi-billion dollar war against non-aggressive, passive "criminals" is as futile as would be outlawing pleasure, and is obviously being met with as much success. And yet despite the continuing failure of their "War on Drugs," politicians, rather than face the facts and consider the alternatives, continue to endorse this unwinnable war as though it were the only conceivable option.

What most people don't seem willing to accept is the fact that part of the cause of substance abuse is our society's very refusal to accept recreational drugs (except for alcohol, Valium and Prozac, of course) into the culture in any reasonable or realistic manner. Instead the general attitude is that of staunch disapproval, as personified by D.A.R.E. and Nancy Reagan's "just say no" campaign.

How are kids supposed to learn anything if all our society does is preach the righteousness of abstinence, tell them that they should just ignore and suppress their natural curiosity? Said approach is really the least effective deterrent (not to mention that for a teenager the forbidden fruit is just that much sweeter); most kids don't respect such authoritarian attitude like they once did—and isn't it a good thing? Well, no, not to everyone it isn't.

Limbaugh's approach to prevention *is* simplicity personified. "How much extra does it cost to have a teacher instruct students not to get involved with drugs? [As if this hasn't already been going on for decades!] What else is there to say? How can there be any debate about that?. . . . We simply tell our kids what they should and should not do. . . ." Limbaugh's sentiments are not uniquely his own—sadly they reflect the mentality of a great number of people.

Simply advocating standards of behavior is the *worst* way by which to keep kids from abusing drugs. If left only to what they are *told* is acceptable, then this more than anything will *misguide* them. Why? Because it is only natural for every individual to look beyond social conventions (if not now then eventually) and look within for guidance, ultimately making their own life decisions.

And when people inevitably make their own choices they'll surely make bad ones if they've never been encouraged to think for themselves, to be the navigator of their own destiny in all circumstances. So when it comes to trying cocaine or heroin, people are that much more likely to make the wrong decision if all they've been taught to do is blindly follow the will of others.

D.A.R.E.'S A JOKE; LET'S GET REAL

The only long-term prevention to drug abuse is through education. Reality-based information and not the laughable scare tactics employed by D.A.R.E. and in health classes, where all drugs get lumped into the same indiscriminate category which preaches that they'll melt your brain and drive you insane.

Drug experimentation isn't wrong onto itself. The real problem begins when those not properly educated begin to experiment—the problem begins when little Johnny takes a puff off a joint with his pals and his mind *doesn't* explode like he's been taught; in fact, maybe he'll find it to be a strange and unusual, pretty darn enjoyable experience. Now how's this kid supposed to believe any other drug info when they've illegalized and demonized this marijuana shit and it clearly isn't all that?

That's when the line becomes dangerously blurred between addictive substances and those drugs whose risk is moderate, and when someone becomes much more willing to experiment with heroin, cocaine, crack, speed, and all that junk. It's like blurring the line between protective and non-protective sex by telling kids that all sex kills unless married as a virgin.

For a drug education to be effective, it's gotta be less preachy. Today's methodology is far too biased toward only teaching about the worst aspects of drugs. If all an education ever does is put emphasis on and highlight the negative aspects, then a person who uses for the first time—like little Johnny—might completely forget about all that bad stuff in lieu of this new positive experience (high). But if the education were more rounded, then they'd be that much more likely to also remember the *negative* stuff. Knowing about a drugs positive effects will make it that much easier for kids to take the negative stuff seriously, to trust this secondhand "truth" given to them by these questionable figures of authority.

Students should be able to take this seriously if they genuinely feel that the education is honest. But most kids today know it *isn't* honest—how can students be expected to trust their teachers when they're so obviously bent towards demonizing all drugs?

Also of fair importance is inspiring students to make their own personal decisions (about things like drug use/experimentation), a notion that's never been exceedingly popular.

Young people shouldn't be dependent on rules or the such to make their minds up for them or shape their awareness, lest it be a strictly limited one. They shouldn't let friends, peers, or authority figures actively guide their actions. Rather, they should be encouraged to decide what's in their own best interest, guiding themselves in doing only that which they truly want and feel right about doing for themselves, for their own pleasure or curiosity.

MARRY ME JANE

The United States has a proud puritanical history of outlawing that deemed impure, even when these things are never substantiated to be a genuine public threat. Booze was banned under the 18th Amendment (1919) and repealed by the 21st Amendment (1933). In 1931 one Harry J. Anslinger was appointed U.S. Commissioner of Narcotics, a man who had helped run the failed Prohibition of alcohol just a short time earlier. Marijuana was then illegalized in 1937 under the Marijuana Tax Stamp Act, only 4 years after Prohibition ended. Just a coincidence? Me thinks not. Those individuals hired under Prohibition needed another enemy, another substance to demonize like they had done to alcohol just 18 years earlier. Since reefer became a popular alternative to alcohol, once Prohibition ended (and with the prompting of greedy pharmaceutical companies) marijuana became a prime target: Public Enemy #1!

Yes, I've smoked the herb. And still do on occasion. I admit that with no shame, nor any insecure pride. It's simply something *I* enjoy to do.

Take it from a guy who once took a few chugs from a bottle of gin, went to the cinema, and ended up puking and passing out three minutes into the feature (*The War of the Roses*—and no, that's not a comment on the movie): marijuana is just as, if not far less, harmful to a person's health than alcohol.

In fact, many, including myself, would argue that the benefits of marijuana (such as industrial and medical, see Appendixes IV & V) far outweigh any benefits derived from alcohol, whereas the downside of alcohol far outweighs that of marijuana. The knowledge is there, I'm not just making this up from my own opinion. People have known this for a long time. In 1988 the DEA's own administrative judge declared that "marijuana is one of the safest, therapeutically active substances known to man." Yet the media is more likely to get some goofball like the Reverend Bud Green as a marijuana legalization advocate (a guy who smokes pot sacramentally to pray to Christ—think Limbaugh's gonna defend this form of "prayer in the classroom"?) as opposed to a reputable representative from Marijuana Policy Project, the National Organization For The Reform of Marijuana Laws, or any group seriously committed to its legalization.

Alcoholism is rampant around the planet *(sexy beer commercials glamorizing drinking!)* and is a real sick addiction, but of all the potheads I've known, only one or two seemed hooked, and even then their "addiction" was quite subtle.

Marijuana certainly *can* be addictive, but it is safe enough that its responsible use is dependent on each individual. Whether genetically predisposed to addiction because of an alcoholic parent or because of psychological problems, many of those who do become addicted are people with addictive personalities. Anything can become addicting. People become addicted to nasal spray! Food can be addictive for some. So whereas, yes, marijuana can be addictive, it is safe enough that people can (and therefore should) be entrusted to make their own choice whether to use much better than the government can make that decision for us.

Probably the worst myth regarding marijuana is that it's gonna lead users to heavier drugs *like* heroin. If someone's craving that higher high to numb their reality; or if they're ignorant of the stark differences between these drugs because of a weakly under-detailed education, then, yeah, I can see that happening.

Other than that, though, it'd be weak to blame someone's experimenting with hard narcotics on weed; do people blame marijuana usage on cigarettes? Look at how many people commit violent crimes while intoxicated; can this be blamed on the alcohol or the person? People who go on to cocaine or heroin might've often blazed a joint, but they probably also downed a little liquor, smoked cigarettes, drank milk, and had had at least one turbulent relationship or occurrence in their life too.

Coincidence? More likely than not, *yes*.

The most serious way marijuana might lead to the use of heavier drugs is simply by virtue of the fact that it's *illegal* like these other substances. Which means that someone who wants to hook up some cheeba might find themselves in an environment laced with all these other drugs, thus making their availability and the temptation to try them that much greater.

Painting crystal-clear distinctions between these substances in the law is far more important than in a classroom, as the society and law are the larger classroom by which most people get a general sense of what's what. Way things are now this line becomes easily blurred, making it that much easier for someone to foolishly cross it and become addicted to a narcotic or stimulant.

But by allowing a legal alternative to alcohol people can enjoy to relieve the pressures of everyday living (besides the pharmaceutical fix many people indulge in to do the same thing), then they'll be reducing the attractiveness people feel towards this subterrane drug-culture within which lies these highly addictive substances, and which marijuana will remain a major part of as long as it remains illegal.

RISKY BUSINESS

Some prudes may argue that even these supposed "recreational" drugs such as marijuana contain an element of risk, don't they? Yes, of course: what a naive question. You should be ashamed for having asked it. Everything in life contains an element of risk—nowadays that includes drinking the water and breathing the air, not to mention the act whose worst repercussion used to just be pregnancy.

The question is, in deciding the law how should the government approach such matters of public safety? When one thinks about it, the answer's almost self-evident. The government should allow citizens the opportunity to do that whose safety or danger depends almost *solely* on the responsibility of the individual. The use of cocaine or heroin has little to do with the responsibility of the individual—I don't care if you're the Pope or the Dalai Lama, almost anyone could and would become easily addicted to these.

Marijuana is a drug that, like alcohol, is not for everyone and can be used dangerously, but whose safe use is still largely dependent on each individual.

Danger is simply an element of *life*. But so long as people continue to deny this, and as long as the great differences between all drugs aren't made perfectly clear, then the path to true danger will continue to be bridged and subsequently crossed, in part because of our refusal to accept manageable risks like marijuana.

I'm not suggesting people start smoking weed for breakfast, lunch and dinner. I'm not talking about endorsing marijuana as this perfectly safe drug to be used frivolously and with carefree abandon; it's definitely NC-18 stuff. Moderation is the key word.

Yes, marijuana can be used to excess. So can alcohol and movie theater popcorn popped in coconut oil. Are we gonna have the government illegalize anything and everything that might be dangerous if used to excess? Do we want them to watch our every step, make our personal decisions, and wipe our backsides for us our entire lives?

I can't speak for anyone else, but am quite confident that I myself prefer not to live a sheltered existence. Open and knowledgeable, OK; but sheltered, ignorant, and afraid of life? Thanks, no.

KICKIN' THA MONKEY

Stimulants and narcotics are by far the sickest substances around, as they're responsible for most of the tragic consequences of drug use. Hopefully use of this dope can be further curved by such educational and legal steps as I just described. But taking measures to prevent use is only half the problem; there are still those already using and those who inevitably will try these drugs, despite all preventative measures. There is still the need to prevent potential addicts by diminishing the street supply.

But how is such a thing done? More cops and more prisons?

Done strategically and efficiently, sure, that might have a *slight* effect on the availability of these drugs. But not much, unless we gain a boost in technology or the funds for such manpower as to guard our borders so thoroughly. As long there's a demand, the supply will never run out in our lifetimes. Therefore the state must do what they can to satisfy the demand just as well, if not better than, they also prevent the supply.

So, what? Just give up and legalize narcotics/stimulants like any other recreational drug?

That's not even an option in my mind. They are far too dangerous. But controlling the drugs is another matter entirely. How? By looking upon and truly accepting addiction as a medical problem, and by treating addicts as such knowing that their addiction will never go away by denying them drugs.

We Yanks would do good to take a cue from our friends across the Atlantic and their policy toward dealing with this dope *shite*. The Mersey Harm Reduction Model in Liverpool, England, is a gradual treatment program wherein addicts can purchase a pharmaceutical fix of the drug they're addicted to. Addiction *is* more than just a mental weakness, it's a physical dependency that often the addict feels absolutely no control over. Trying to keep the drugs away from addicts is pointless—most such drugs come here to go to full-time customers; but then of course there's always some left over for the first-time user. And then addicts may themselves turn friends or acquaintances on to their drug habit. Which is why the primary concern is their availability to the novice dope-fiend. And the only way to substantially diminish this street supply is by ebbing the addict's demand from the street into pharmaceutical addiction-treatment programs.

The idea of such a program may sound somewhat radical, when in fact we've had a similar program in effect here for a couple decades: it's called a methadone clinic. Course, methadone was meant to help free heroin users from their addiction, not support it. The program's a miserable failure, though—very few get off heroin because of it, and many of those who do end up getting addicted to methadone instead.

Establishment of an addiction-treatment program similar to the Mersey Harm Reduction Model would allow addicts to function in their everyday life until they seek treatment, and would keep the street-demand low so that potential first-time users won't be able to find the drugs as easily.

ECONOMICS 101:
PROHIBITION = CRIME

Medicalization of addiction would also have significant repercussions in the crime rate. You'd have to be seriously defunct in your mental capacities indeed not to make some basic connection between all the crime and gang activity taking place in our country and these drugs, not to link much of the violence happening in our streets directly or subsequently to the incredible amount of revenue such substances generate. The money created by demand for these drugs—billions upon billions—strongly fuels crime and gang activity, revenue that keeps this way of life appealing.

When alcohol was illegalized, what happened? It boosted the rise of crime and violence, bribery and corruption in local government. It was the best thing that ever happened to mobsters like Al Capone. When Prohibition ended, crime certainly didn't end with it, but legalization did take this power of supply and demand, of all this money, out of the hands of criminals.

It's not premature to assume that the illegal drug market today is far richer than the moonshine market during Prohibition, and that the element of crime today is much wider spread than the organized gangs of that era. And thus it is equally fair to assume that, were this drug demand and supply better dealt with, if this drug revenue were taken away from the criminal element, the impact on crime in this country would be wide-reaching.

In fact, if I had to attribute the deterioration of our inner cities to specific causes, drug prohibition would certainly be one of the largest and most profound contributing factors. The legalization of marijuana and the medicalization of addiction won't end *all* these problems, but at the very least it would soften the lure and attractiveness of a life of crime, for which such drug revenue is an absolutely *enormous* part of.

FEASIBILITY

Even if the reader agrees this to be a good idea in theory, many may argue that Middle America will never accept such realism, but will continue to oppose drugs on broad based ideals. But we control our culture, and this kind of dramatic change *is* possible. People must be educated. If enough people come to this same realization, this can occur.

But then again, there are strong, discouraging cues in our society all the time.

U.S. Surgeon General Jocelyn Elders was fired by Clinton, little more than a month after Republicans swept the '94 House and Senate elections, supposedly because she said something about masturbation. Were it truly that remark for which she was fired, then this would excellently demonstrate how I believe she wasn't fired for *what* she said so much as *how* she said it. She didn't always express herself quite as eloquently as most politicians feel comfortable with, and I'd even go so far as to say she seemed to have something of a mild speech impediment. She certainly left herself open for misinterpretation with her masturbation comment.

Speaking at an AIDS function, she said, "As per your specific question in regard to masturbation, I think that . . . it's a part of something that perhaps should be taught."

Perhaps Jocelyn Elders wasn't the best Surgeon General; some of her comments regarding Catholics having "a love affair with fetuses" were particularly poorly-expressed. Other than that bit of ugliness, though, she was a tremendous breath of fresh air, the way she recommended the government examine the prospect of drug legalization, which surely was one of the main reasons she was *actually* fired. When Elders suggested that they look into the theoretical possibility of "legalizing" drugs, the Clinton administration tried to distance itself from her as much as possible, and politicians in both parties scurried like the popularity-poll worshipping cockroaches they are when you flip the kitchen light on after dark.

Prior to election '96, President Clinton put forth his own drug plan, beginning with the groundbreaking idea of "encouraging young people to reject drugs." After Clinton's speech, Gen. Barry McCaffrey (the federal drug policy coordinator) said, "There is no reason why we can't return America to a 1960s level, pre-Vietnam era level of drug use." Are these guys delusional? Even more recently Clinton encouraged Hollywood to produce more responsible entertainment. "Never glorify drugs, but more importantly, tell our children the truth. Show them that drug use is really a death sentence." Ah yes, the truth. Something Washington politicians and Hollywood producers have a real mastery of.

You might have noticed the almost complete lack of mention of Limbaugh in this chapter. That's because while I very easily could've found numerous examples of his and other conservatives anti-drug sentiments to nit-pick over, these views are so incredibly simplistic it didn't seem to serve any legitimate purpose to do so. Nancy Reagan coined the simplicity of the stance. And so I figured, why waste valuable time chronicling Limbaugh's redundant feelings towards the prospect of such drug legalization? His position goes without saying, and anything I write on the subject is by default a direct opposition to said position.

So long as "just say no" remains our societal norm, people will continue to use nonchalantly, and the crime and many subsequent problems will persist without end.

Sincere drug education, marijuana legalization, and addiction medicalization is what poses to help solve many of these problems. More people might be tokin' the chronic, but in the long run I believe such legal and educational steps would trigger a significant decline in the use of narcotics and stimulants—and what's more, would allow those who experiment to do so more aware and knowledgeable about what exactly they're getting themselves into.

A LITTLE
SOMETHING ON
ANIMAL COMPASSION

In *The Way Things Ought to Be*, in a chapter on the animal rights "wackos," Limbaugh essentially said animals don't deserve and shouldn't have any rights because they don't have the power to claim them. When first I read this, my gut impulse was to retort: The Africans that were enslaved didn't have the power to claim their rights at the time either, does that make what was done to them *right*? Is he simply saying might makes right?

But really I know Limbaugh *is* right. He's simply stating a fact. Under our law animals have no rights except as human property. He is also stating an opinion, that animals should have no rights in our law. I'm not going to argue with him on that point. Considering the mindset of most humans on animal rights, it'd be absurd to argue for giving animals protection under the law the same as for humans. It's just not a realistic point to argue on, and accomplishes little towards broadening people's capacity for treasuring the life on this planet for itself and of their own free will. Those "animal rights" organizations that advocate such equal legal protection may be of good intention, but their unrealistic approach to the issue often only reaffirms the position of the majority of people who simply in no way see animals anywhere near as equals to ourselves.

For myself this isn't an issue of legal rights, but of moral compassion, of voluntarily choosing not to murder our fellow creatures simply out of the goodness of our own hearts. And it is that which I would have to take exception with Limbaugh, his conviction that not only should animals have no rights, but that neither do they deserve any compassion for the innate sanctity of their life. Because "animals and everything else are subspecies whose position on the planet is subordinate to that of humans."

PASSIONLESS COMPASSION

Limbaugh tries to soften his position that animals can have no legal rights by lamely trying to make it sound as though he does have compassion. ". . . before you jump to the conclusion that I am a callous, insensitive, and a heartless animal-hater, hear me out. Before beginning the discussion of rights, let me make it perfectly clear that my belief that animals don't have rights is not equivalent to saying that human beings have no moral obligation to protect animals when they can." Later: "Humans have a responsibility toward lower species and must treat them humanely. *Humanely*, now that's an interesting term. Doesn't that mean as a human would like to be treated? Why not treat them animally? Because that would mean killing them." "[Animals] tear each other from limb to limb." But wait a second, I've never heard of killer cattle eating other animals, nor have I heard of chickens, pigs, or sheep engaging in such murder and mayhem. So how could treating them animally mean killing them when these animals don't even kill each other? And yet we *do* kill these animals, which, according to the logic of Limbaugh's statement, means *we* are the ones acting *animally* in our treatment of these animals.

To conclusively show just what an uncallous, sensitive, and a hearty animal-lover he is, Limbaugh says we have a responsibility not to slaughter any animal to the point of extinction (what a guy!). As a specific example, he says we "should not allow elephants to become extinct just so a few people can have ivory carvings." But so long as the elephants are herded in wildlife parks and it profits the surrounding population, he sees nothing wrong with killing a set number of elephants for their tusks and hides. He says animal rights wackos only want to "attack the American way of life" and "obstruct human progress". It's obvious he has no respect for these animals outside how they can profit mankind.

Limbaugh does not believe humans have a "moral obligation" to protect animals when they can; he believes they have a responsibility to prevent extinction so they may continue to slaughter these animals for their own self-interest. That's clearly his position, no matter how disingenuously he dresses it up as compassion.

THE
"MY BRAIN'S BIGGER THAN YOUR BRAIN"
EXCUSE

The reason animals are held in such low esteem is because of the traditional view that man and man alone is a rational animal. Limbaugh points out that only recently has there been any acceptance of the opposing view that all animals have intelligence, and mostly among scientists and the educated classes (those pesky scientists and educated people—they think they're so much smarter than the rest of us).

Actually, the view that animals have intelligence isn't necessarily one of education, but of basic observation. All one need do is observe animals to note that they think about what they do. Granted what they do is usually limited to base necessities of living, but their actions are clearly the result of thought. Just because those thoughts are formed as a result of stimuli from the natural world around and within them in no way lessens the reality of the individual thought process all living creatures engage in.

But Limbaugh would have us believe these animals are like machines simply reacting to preprogrammed instructions, citing some brain who concedes bees make hives, birds make nests, and beavers make dams, but those productions are purely "instinctive." So, what, when a man cuts down trees and builds a house this is the product of rational thought (even though it may be a skill that's been passed down from generation to generation), but when a beaver cuts down some trees and builds a dam it's just acting on instinct? Well then, what prompted that *human* to build a house? To protect himself from the natural elements, for self-preservation—isn't this in and of itself an instinctive tendency?

There's no denying that humans are infinitely smarter than the smartest animal below us, but I don't see why this needs to make Limbaugh take the position that we're the *only* creature capable of reason. Man may indeed be the only animal capable of complex thought, but we're also the only one who becomes consumed with arrogance and insecurity. Limbaugh actually seems *threatened* by the idea that animals may possess some basic element of intelligence.

For reasons unclear to me, Limbaugh appears to consider love the rarest of commodities which can only be spread so thin. This is the only explanation I can figure for why he believes humans can't love animals more without this causing us to love ourselves less. He asserts that animal rights crusaders are only out to *devalue* human life, accuses them of holding a "fundamental premise that animals are superior to human beings" and speaks of protecting ourselves "in this war for dominance of the planet".

Clearly the workings of a rational, superior mind.

As yet more proof of animals worthless inferiority, Limbaugh quotes the same brain (Mortimer Adler) as saying: "In making houses, bridges, or any other of their artifacts, men invent and select. They are truly artists, as animals are not." Yes, people make *things* to clutter up our lives because we're a somewhat intelligent species . . . but are one's creations and collections of *things* that by which we judge the value of their life? I can think of no artist who thrills or inspires me like that of our natural world and its many inhabitants.

SUCCULENT SOUL

As someone presently living in a household with three cats, I can tell you all animals have their own quirks and personalities. And these cats *are* intelligent. They're also very needy and whine a lot. I would sincerely compare the intelligence of these cats to that of a human infant; often having a pet feels like having a smaller, less dependent child. My cats have the same playful innocence and intelligence of a small child, while having the survival instinct of an adult. They may not know the intellectual difference between "right and wrong," but they know pleasure and pain, they know love and hate. They're not capable of such hostility that the difference between right and wrong is even necessarily something they'd need to be able to distinguish between like us more violence-prone humans. They exude a natural capacity for love, and embody a childlike innocence and purity of soul, that simply leaves me in awe. The same could easily be said of dogs, and of just about all other animals.

How the casual, everyday slaughter of these beautiful creatures can have no impact on the conscious of those who support such murder is beyond me to comprehend. Rush says, "I've never killed an animal, I never intend to kill one." But there is no difference between purchasing an animal product and killing the animal yourself. They wouldn't have killed it unless they thought someone was going to buy it. Supply and demand. Maybe that's why so few people feel any compassion for this death—because in our industrialized society very few people actually have to witness or commit these acts of murder. Once upon a time people killed their dinner themselves and gave direct thanks for the "sacrifice" of that life (which I might have a grain of respect for), whereas people today have been so removed from this that they view meat as simply another economic product.

HOLY HYPOCRISY, FATMAN!

There exists a most troubling paradox as to why it's morally acceptable to kill all the other creatures inferior to ourselves. Because most people—such as Limbaugh—present two separate arguments that irrefutably contradict each other. On the one hand they point out that these animals (or some of them—usually the ones nobody eats) are already killing one another.

The second argument is that this murder is justified because animals are so dumb, because we're so much more intelligent than they. First we point to the animals and say, "Our actions are no worse than theirs," then we point to ourselves and proclaim, "And we're also so much smarter." Don't people see the inherent contradiction there?

We claim to be civilized and then excuse our actions by comparing them to those of the animals we've killed. Whereas if we were *truly* as intelligent and civilized as we like to believe, we'd hold ourselves to higher standards of morality than the animals we willfully kill.

Get it?

Intelligence is not the ability to kill all the other animals below us, that is sheer might and not excusable onto itself; intelligence is the ability to recognize this power of ours and not use it because we know better. That is what distinguishes the greatest mankind can achieve with the natural naiveté most other animals seem to possess; not our ability to kill just because we can, but our ability to control and respect and feel humility before this great power.

THEY SAY THIS EARTH IS A
BAD MOTHER—SHUT YOUR MOUTH!
JUST TALKIN' ABOUT EARTH—
CAN YA DIG IT?

Limbaugh declares: "There is no one who wants to fix [damage to the environment] more than I do." What does he believe is the key to cleaning up and protecting our environment? ". . . unfettered free enterprise . . ." that's what. He believes environmentalists are only out to "attack the American way of life [and] punish people for simply being themselves" and that citizens will demand a cleaner environment without any *big government* intervention.

As a prime example of citizens taking care of and protecting the environment themselves, Limbaugh mentioned the time in 1969 the Cuyahoga River—just downstream of Cleveland—became so polluted it actually caught fire, and "the people" rolled up their sleeves and cleaned it up themselves. Sure, as Limbaugh begrudgingly concedes, "some regulation was used [*some?*], but the major factor was good old American know-how."

What in the hell *is this guy talking about?!* Unfettered free enterprise is the key to a clean environment, and the American people will deal with this pollution themselves if and when it gets too extreme (like, say, large bodies of water *catching on fire*)?

Limbaugh says: "The more economic growth we have, the more a prosperous people will demand a clean environment." But what if demanding a clean environment threatened their very prosperity? It is for this reason that corporations cannot be allowed to self-regulate their own pollutants. And yet this blazingly obvious *conflict of interest* goes unnoticed by Limbaugh, who feels a corporation's success will prompt them to suddenly *care* about the environment. But if they were interested in the consequences of their actions, they wouldn't have polluted the environment to begin with! Success won't cause them to feel a sense of responsibility; their ever-growing greed will weaken any lingering reserve of responsibility they may have left.

Limbaugh acts as though regulation were an unwarranted and malicious assault against free enterprise. But businesses still have the freedom to make and sell products for profit. It is *because* we have free enterprise, and because this breeds greed, that it's necessary for our government to control the inevitable pollution.

But Limbaugh says, "What [environmentalists] want to do is attack our way of life. Their primary enemy: capitalism." And that "environmentalists paint humans as an aberration; as the natural enemy of nature." Using the most broad of condemnations, Limbaugh hastily dismisses environmentalism as another crackpot scheme of those foul anti-Americans—"liberals"—who mean to undermine capitalism.

Limbaugh can't see the forest for the broccoli between his ears.

The very nature of capitalism, of free enterprise and free trade, is something which puts a person's lust for money and for power at threat to override their better sense of responsibility. The law exists because human nature is not something that can be completely trusted. That's because, as any thinking being can see, humanity is capable of horrific cruelty and cold indifference. So how can these greedy corporations be trusted to treat the environment right when humans can't even be trusted to behave morally amongst themselves?

And think about it: are the laws meant to protect people against robbery, assault, rape or murder encroachments on their freedoms? No, they are the *source* of their freedom. There is no freedom in lawlessness—only anarchy in which humans are free to demonstrate just how sick and cruel their natures can be. Why then does Limbaugh suggest that regulation is an encroachment against free enterprise? With the freedom to produce practically whatever they want, how can

Limbaugh insist that the private sector should be entrusted to dispense of their pollutants responsibly?

Government regulation isn't a hindrance toward capitalism, it's an intrinsic *necessity* of it.

Imagine our country is the house in which we live. Now if some of the inhabitants of this house begin throwing all sorts of crude garbage about, what should the head of the house do? Simply wait for them to clean it up when they felt like it, if ever? I believe keeping our house clean is a little more important than any inconvenience this may cause those who are forced to be responsible for their own waste products and pollutants.

Limbaugh asserts that nothing a scientist says which doesn't sound rational to *him* probably isn't true. He honestly believes that his "common sense" is a more accurate and truthful perspective, lens onto reality, than the scientist's outlook on the world (not spiritual or mental, but the *physical world*). He dismisses scientific experts and mountains of scientific evidence by contending, among other things, that fossil-fuel emissions and chlorofluorocarbons do not pollute the air or contribute to the greenhouse effect; that there's never been a man-made cause of depletion in the ozone layer; that big business pollution poses no threat to the environment; and that there's no need for the dismantling of nuclear weapons. (I'm pretty much convinced that if he were unable to see the hidden image in one of those Magic Eye 3-D stereograms, he'd claim it didn't exist and that those who said it did were a bunch of drug-induced liberals.)

According to Limbaugh, environmental "wackos" want everyone to retrograde to a time when the life expectancy was 54.9 years. Without question the advancements which have improved our life expectancy are good, such as medicine and sanitation. (Life expectancy also went up because of healthier diets—though I doubt Limbaugh would know that, what with him getting annoyed at any news regarding the cholesterol content of popcorn or the dangers of undercooked meat!) But what do pollutants, chemicals or emissions have to do with our life expectancy? These things are *threats* to the quality of our lives, not the source of them. Limbaugh seems to think anything which helps the economy is justifiable. This is his excuse for disregarding the environment: because the pillage of it reaps many financial rewards, and to a conservative like Limbaugh nothing is the bottom line more than the bottom line.

TREES ARE NOT A CROP

There is hardly a more clear and evident example of this tendency of Limbaugh's to value the paper more than the tree it was derived from (especially when that paper is painted green and called *money*) than his attitude toward the limber industry. One of his '35 Undeniable Truths of Life' is that: "The most beautiful thing about a tree is what you do with it after you cut it down."

No matter what your appreciation for their many industrial uses, trees are most definitely *not* a crop, as Limbaugh has said. For starters, a crop isn't something one must pick at sparingly, thoughtful of its place in the big picture of things; for unlike crops, forests play an important part in our planet's atmosphere, the cycle of oxygen to carbon dioxide/carbon dioxide to oxygen.

Trees also cannot be planted and cultivated in a single season like most things considered a crop (fruits, vegetables, herbs, tobacco). Trees don't exactly grow that fast, in case you hadn't noticed. And so to suggest that clear-cutting can do no harm because the timber industry is also planting new trees means very little in the end if the rate at which they are cutting down forests eventually exceeds the rate of growth for a new tree. The more the population explodes, the more the timber industry is going to convince the government it's justified in clearing all our old-growth forests.

But Limbaugh, being the great admirer of nature that he is, doesn't see what the difference is between old-growth forests and those only recently planted. "What the environmentalists are saying . . . [is that trees] that have been planted by man are not as worthy or valuable as those that grow in 'virgin' forests. What is a virgin forest anyway? Most trees live for only a couple hundred years and then die." If Limbaugh ever ventured further than a few kilometers from the nearest Dairy

Queen, he might know that virgin forests are those untouched by man, whose trees can date back over a millenium. And unlike humans, trees never stop growing. And so yes, even from a logger's standpoint, old-growth trees *are* more valuable than new ones. Not only can they yield far more wood, but their beauty and grandeur is incomparable to trees which are cleared every thirty years—like something whose only value is measured in terms of greenback.

Limbaugh purports that there's as much acreage of forest today as when the Constitution was written (as proof he cites a book which favorably compares today's acreage with that in *1920*). What is it that motivates him to make such clearly dubious claims? Is it because Limbaugh finds trees unpleasant to behold; are they offensive to his senses? Does he take pleasure in envisioning a treeless landscape? Or is it simply the employment of loggers and the profits of logging companies he's defending?

Truly it is noble, the way Limbaugh looks out for the best interest of laborers above all else. It is also somewhat distressing, the way he pays absolutely no mind to the consequences of that labor. Never mind the damage that is wrought, so long as people have jobs, mundane as they may typically be, then everything's fine and dandy. It's capitalist fanaticism at its blindest.

This all-consuming faith in the saving grace of the almighty dollar is the only reason I can think of to explain his animosity towards so-called "tree huggers." And why it is that whenever a group protests the clear-cutting of a forest, even if it's just local community folk who've enjoyed the land as a public park for years, Limbaugh goes out of his way to showcase video of some wild soul (who obviously took a little too much *something* back in the '60s) rambling away like a lunatic as an argument for saving the forest. Ha ha, look at the spaced-out hippie and his tree-hugging friends—yup, you can always count on Limbaugh to back his arguments up with illustrious examples of his own cunning and refinement.

Obviously trees are not so sacred they should never be chopped down. (Though frankly the thought of all the trees sacrificed in the production of this book makes my stomach churn.) But the short-lived wealth of logging companies should not take precedence over the vitality of our natural surroundings. The boundaries for timber land must be made crystalline—the logging industry's profit margin cannot be justification for reducing all of our nation's old-growth forests into unsightly *croplands*.

OUR FRIGHTENING VULNERABILITY

Aside from the slow self-poisoning of mass consumerism and "unfettered free enterprise," there's also the potential for accidental catastrophes, such as with nuclear reactors. Chernobyl is one example (and Three Mile Island another) to take serious caution from—it didn't just kill numerous people, but the radiation also made a lot of people sick and *deformed* the newborn children and subsequent offspring of those who lived nearby and survived it.

Let us all hope that eventually the human race becomes clever enough to find alternate sources of power with which to feed our electrical addictions.

And then there's the world war-machine. It is within the military, terrorist factions, and in the careless name of science that still more great threats lie. As things are going now around our world, it seems an inevitability of time that some horrendous accidents or acts of terrorism or flat-out war will pose serious threats to parts of our planet. I say that not to frighten people, but to alert them to what to me seems like an obvious and ominous reality.

How can Limbaugh say something so intentionally careless as, "There is only one way to get rid of nuclear weapons—use them." How can Limbaugh honestly say he doesn't see any possibility of humans to destroy life on Earth? Knowing of all our nuclear power, knowing that the neutron, hydrogen and atom bomb exist, along with chemical warfare and synthetically produced diseases, how can anyone say they don't see our potential to destroy the environment? Or of simply destroying *ourselves*?

The human species has existed for roughly the bat of an eye in terms of evolution, and yet the explosion of industry and technology has taken place largely within the last hundred years. That's nothing! And yet we've already got nuclear reactors and their byproducts everywhere—don't people see the potential for this power we've only recently discovered to blow up in our faces?

No, technology/science is not inherently evil. Nor is it all good. It is an incredible physical power, the likes of which has never knowingly been in the hands of humans before, and it can improve our lives just as easily destroy them. It's a matter of responsibility, understanding, control; things we are far from fully possessing.

Rush is right: man can never re-create the power of nature, nor can man destroy the planet. But then it's not a question of destroying the planet; it's a matter of destroying the environment that nurtures and supports the life on this planet, ourselves sadly being the most advanced species to speak for. Even the concept of killing all humans is not easy to envision—it seems that no matter what catastrophe occurred, somewhere humans would manage to survive like the cucarachas we are. But in what form, and for how much longer?

My own fear is that only when our planet is ravished to the point where it seriously threatens everybody's well being will the masses come to the defense of the environment. And by then it might be too little too late. If only people appreciated this lonely little planet as the splendid oasis of life it is, as the physical whole from which we are born, then they'd gratefully defend it for its own sake, and not just as a desperate last effort to save *ourselves*.

Clearly we need not be ashamed to champion the environment, for it is the most valuable physical resource we have next to our own lives, far more valuable than our little pieces of monetary. This is the realization people should, but ultimately will need to make for self-preservation, and the direction with which our environment we should be in tune.

CREATION BEYOND *WHOSE* UNDERSTANDING?

Until such a time, however, people will continue to exploit and rape the environment, because humans can never re-create the power of nature; humans can never destroy the planet; and the way we're living is perfectly natural.

Or, what Limbaugh really means to say, man is no match for *God*. Limbaugh's belief that mankind could never possibly destroy the environment is basically his way of kneeling down before the mythological one. This view is nothing more than the objective manifestation of his feeling of inferiority before all that which he doesn't understand and claims is beyond understanding, that which he conveniently attributes to God.

Subsequently Limbaugh feels there should be no restrictions on how businesses dispense of their waste products. His attitude is that environmentalists are nothing more than ninny-ninny worry warts who believe "the world's gonna come to an end." And just as animals are ours to slaughter to the point of *extinction*, Limbaugh similarly feels that—since chances of the entire world ending seems unlikely—it's perfectly reasonable then to carelessly pollute the planet in our monetary pursuits. The environment is expendable because the Earth is indestructible. I can only assume this arrogance is based on his fanatical belief in the Biblical myth of Creation, his conviction that God made this world as is solely for the exploitation of mankind.

How else could I explain this uncanny disdain of his?

Then again, he doesn't exactly appear to worship his own body; it's not quite a temple. So maybe it's not surprising he has so little respect or understanding for our Earth's body. (*D'oh*—there I go again.)

FEMINISM

OR:

WOMEN COPING IN A
MALE DOMINATED, SEXIST WORLD

It's no coincidence that the chapter in Limbaugh's first book entitled *Feminism And The Culture War* begins by citing examples of extremism—a feminist who wants the abolition of marriage and another who doesn't believe women can be fully feminine unless they recognize themselves as lesbians—and then states: "It is from this perspective that I want to share with you the following thoughts on feminism." More than just being annoyed by a few instances of extremism, it's clear Limbaugh's exploiting radicals to tarnish the very idea of feminism. (Much the way he uses the extremists to dismiss just about any movement he disagrees with.)

Like environmentalists and other *wackos*, Limbaugh conveniently disregards feminism as another radical faction of the Socialist Utopians. He says that "feminism is another of those vehicles to transport unpopular liberalism into mainstream society. . . . [liberals] have decided to repackage those ideas in more politically palatable gift wrapping, and feminism is one of those packages."

But Limbaugh's characterization of feminism is so inconsistent, it often rings less of liberal bashing than as the bitter fumings of a fatass scorned. In both his original and his updated '35 Undeniable Truths of Life,' Limbaugh said feminism was created to allow ugly women access to the mainstream of society. And yet in his first book he wrote, "The original concerns of feminists, such as equal pay for equal work, were laudable and justifiable. People had a right to be upset at the treatment some women received, and some of their activism and protests were understandable." Well, since obviously women—beautiful, ugly or plain—weren't a part of the workforce until after the rights secured to them by the women's movement, saying that feminism was created to allow ugly women access to the mainstream can only be construed as his backhanded (and rather cowardly) way of calling all feminists ugly. And if that isn't the acerbic fury of a fatass scorned, then I don't know what is.

Limbaugh also makes constant references to *feminazis*. When I first heard him using this reference, I wasn't all that offended, and on a certain level thought it was pretty true. There *are* feminist radicals out there, just as there are radicals in every aspect of life. (There may even be some conservatives more extreme than Rush—ya think?) It's just a fact of life that there are good people and bad people, smart people and stupid people, and without fail this axiom proves true with every religious group, political party, or social movement.

But Limbaugh implies that *all* feminists are extremists, and tries to paint the portrait that your average, sensible woman wants nothing to do with that crazy movement altogether. He writes: "It's not what most women want. *Time* magazine reports that 63 percent of American women reject the feminist label."

Had Limbaugh not been so busy misinterpreting this to support his own groundless assertion, he might have noticed that *Time* claims these women specifically reject the feminist *label*, not the feminist movement. Huge difference. I myself reject the liberal label, but there's no denying my views lean towards what some would classify "the left." The feminist label has come to represent those who belong to a specific group or organization; most women do not belong to such, and so it's not surprising they would reject this label.

The majority of women in this country may not embrace the feminist label or organizations, but it'd be naive to believe most aren't supportive of and involved in the women's movement in their own personal everyday way.

THE BIG SQUEEZE

Sexual harassment accusations are typically frivolous, and all the hyperbole the issue's been given is only a growing inconvenience for men to have to be more self-conscious about what we do and say while in the workplace. Or so would roughly appear to be Limbaugh's sensitive position on the issue.

Limbaugh claims sexual harassment "has poisoned relations between the sexes." And that sexual harassment's "exploitation by feminists who seek to advance their political agenda has resulted in total confusion and chaos." Limbaugh gives an example of the fallout: "Men can no longer enjoy themselves or tell jokes with a lot of women around, because anything they say within the earshot of women can be construed as sexual harassment."

But the fact is everybody must take personal responsibility for their own behavior while in public, especially a forced social situation like at work. Seems some guys would prefer to preserve the workplace as their own private Good Ol' Boys club wherein they can be just as rude, crude, and nasty as they like. Get with the times you geezers.

And even assuming that charges of sexual harassment *are* frequently frivolous, to claim this as proof that it's been blown out of proportion makes little sense when you consider how many frivolous lawsuits abound in regard to police brutality, prison abuse, and product liability. What area of the law *don't* frivolous lawsuits abound in? This hardly means that the seriousness of these things has been exaggerated; frivolous lawsuits are simply the price we pay for living in a society with due process of law. Better that than living in a country where things like sexual harassment, police brutality, and harm caused by careless corporations aren't taken seriously at all.

Limbaugh, however, suggests that sexual harassment is so frivolous and trivial a problem that it should be allowed to take place *unhindered* by any burdensome laws. "I want people to get along with one another, without making a legal case out of everything. . . . It bothers me no end, especially when so many people think the government should intervene to solve these things."

Limbaugh concluded his sexual harassment argument by pointing out that men and women are *(gasp!)* different. The truly odd thing about his conviction of the great differences between the sexes is that, at the same time, he denounces the idea that women might somehow contribute something *different* than men in the governing process.

While addressing some pro-choice rally, Vice-President Al Gore said, "For quite a long time most political systems around the world have been overbalanced toward a distinctively male way of interpreting the world." Limbaugh didn't only believe this statement was wrong, he thought it was downright *weird*, that Gore was pandering to feminists who are setting themselves up as victims. This from the same guy who, after admitting to getting off on a dirty phone call, wrote: "It just proves how men and women instinctively and naturally look at events differently. . . . It's always been this way. It's a beautiful thing." So women look at things differently when it comes to dirty phone calls but *not* in regard to politics or matters of state? Or their right to an abortion? Or when it comes to the appropriateness of sex jokes in the workplace?

G.I. JANE vs JABBA THE HUTT

My own pedestrian observations as to the differences between the sexes is that males seem more naturally aggressive, more physical in the way they interact with the world around them. Women, on the other hand, seem more naturally nurturing, more verbal and emotional in how they interact. This isn't to say men aren't capable of child-rearing; nor that women aren't capable of hard labor, such as in the military or as firefighters.

But we should expect these women to be rather exceptional specimens; nor does this mean, as some extremists have suggested, that the physical strength and endurance tests should be reduced for women. Those women who wish to enter these demanding professions should have to prove their strength just like *anyone* applying for such a job; for tasks like putting out fires or engaging in military combat, you only want the most qualified people for the job—there's no room for affirmative action for the physically weak.

Limbaugh conveniently talks out of both sides of his rather large mouth when it comes to women fighting in combat. First he says: "Women have played a very powerful role in civilizing men. . . . It is not to say that this has been their only role or that they should not have an identity apart from men." But then later he explains that women shouldn't be allowed to fight in combat because: "Women have definite societal roles that are crucial to the continuation of mankind." Huh? He says it's bad enough there are men coming home in body bags, must we put women in them as well?

So, what, it's unacceptable to see women coming home in body bags compared to men? This almost suggests he views men coming home this way as acceptable . . . but women in body bags, no, now *that'd* be going too far?! You wanna know something, I view the deaths of women or men exactly alike: with complete disgust. But, sickened as I am by such violence, it's an unfortunate fact that "to attain peace we must prepare for war," and people are inevitably going to die in the duties of our military. What difference does the gender of the fallen soldier make? If American women want to fight and, yes, possibly die for their country, then why not afford them this?

Limbaugh might argue it only illustrates his tremendous love for women that he doesn't want them dying in military combat. But I suspect this view of his is actually much more crude and condescending. More likely explanation is that it just breaks his heart to think of those fertile women dying overseas in the military when they could be back home popping out babies and fulfilling their crucial role in "the continuation of mankind."

CONCLUSION

It's been my experience that a fair number of individuals—mostly white males—become very uncomfortable discussing our country's history of sexism and racism. They feel that any attempt to confront these issues is equivalent to placing all the blame on their doorstep. And so, rather than accept these realities as fact, their irrational feelings of guilt prompt them to deny that such prejudice is even an issue worthy of discussion.

Not to make any kind of overt comparison—but if the metaphor fits—maybe people do this for the same reason many fascists deny the Holocaust took place: because it makes them look bad and weakens support for their party. Perhaps the reason some conservatives don't want to openly acknowledge this still-existent sexism, or racism, is because it's rooted in the same schools of traditional thought they so cherish. (Though of course the beliefs underlying "conservatism" have become a little more Disneyfied here in America compared to their Old World roots.)

There's no question that great strides have been made in equalizing the sexes; and yes, like all movements, feminism has been taken to extremes by specific individuals. But we must bear in mind that these changes, and these attempts at change, have been in effect collectively for such a limited time. For less than a hundred years this movement has attempted to overcome *thousands of years* of deeply rooted, institutionalized sexism.

There are numerous people in positions of power and authority still strongly against women's political and economic rights. And that's just here in the United States—that's to say nothing of all the cultures around the world which remain *extremely* prejudiced toward women as ineffectual and worthless compared to men.

And so of course this is gonna be a gradual and steady progression, not something that's resolved overnight. It's come a long way so far, just think of how much further it can go. You think the state of things *now* are much improved over yesteryears past?—just imagine how much greater our awareness of the basic equality between the sexes can grow in the years to come, in this country and around the world.

That's why I say today's "women's movement" (whatever name it goes by or embodiment it takes) has not overstayed its welcome, and, despite what Limbaugh seems to want everyone to believe, is still a positive cause to be stalwartly supported.

A MATTER OF
PERSPECTIVE

I'm going to talk about abortion now. Not 'cause it's something I care deeply for or think about that often, but because it's there, and it's an issue we're all gonna have to reckon with sooner or later. Not to mention that it's complicated as all heck. When approaching this, I realize there's no way to be honest about how I feel without coming across like I view life as cheap. By the time they're done reading this I'm sure there are many conservatives who will think me to be the devil incarnate. That's a risk I'm willing to take, though, for it's important those in support of "choice" begin an honest moral discussion on abortion—unpleasant journey to the dark side as it may prove to be. . . .

The heart of the pro-life argument regards the rights of the unborn. Limbaugh writes: ". . . once [abortion advocates] concede that a fetus is life anytime before birth, they've lost the argument." The argument's barely begun. *Roe vs. Wade* may indeed be bad constitutional law. I'm not knowledgeable enough about the law to argue in those terms. But I am more than willing to admit that a newborn is life from embryo through fetus, and still willing to argue for abortion.

Besides the notion that life has no definite beginning or end but for our primitive perceptions of birth and death, human life obviously begins at conception. You know, when the mother and father do a bit of the old nasty. But from conception, that life-form grows inside the woman and is a *part* of her body, as she feeds it with the food she eats and subjects it to the tobacco, alcohol, and drugs she uses while pregnant.

Limbaugh alleges that abortion isn't about the individual rights of a mother, and that women can't be allowed to do whatever they want with their bodies. His rationalization: "Can a woman choose to steal, using her own body? Of course not. Can she choose to do drugs? Not according to the law. Can she legally choose to be a prostitute? Again, no, which establishes, as does the drug example, that there is precedent for society determining what a woman can and can't do with her body."

He's quite correct. But is there a limit to what the government can tell a woman to do with her body? If a woman is pregnant, should she not be allowed to drink? After all, everything she consumes is likewise consumed by her child, and it's illegal to give alcohol to children. Should a pregnant woman who has the occasional cocktail be arrested on the grounds of contributing to the delinquency of a minor? Or of putting her fetus at risk? Of course not. Thus establishing that a woman's rights over her body cannot be completely subservient to the life she carries inside herself.

This is not an easy line to define. The very fact that it's illegal to get an abortion in the third trimester collaborates the precedence of determining what women do to their bodies—in the most sensible regions of my heart, mind and soul I believe such to be of sound reason. And yet when only a couple weeks old, no larger than a peanut, the aborting of a newly-conceived embryo doesn't much bother me.

Am I only fooling myself, seeing the new life-form for less than it is simply because of its superficial size? What's the difference between that embryo and fetus that one should be protected from murder and the other shouldn't?

Depends entirely on your perspective, of course.

No matter what its *size*, I have no problem seeing either embryo or an old person, or for that matter an insect as life sprung forth from the same essential source. Now this hardly means I feel the same when a human dies as when someone steps on an ant, as it's difficult to imagine that anything so minuscule could feel or know so much as for the ending of their life to be such a tragic thing. But as the life-form develops into a more complex creature, and is more aware and sensitive to this physical world, the more I feel for its right to life, while still seeing it as just another beautiful creation, like myself or that ant. Or that embryo.

Can abortion seriously be seen as murder when the embryo is so underdeveloped and insensitive to its physical body? Sure it can, just as purposely stepping on an ant can be said to be murder. It's the taking of a life, but we must perceive it from a more *physical* perspective.

Limbaugh makes the argument that, hey, that aborted life could have been the next Beethoven, they could be the person who invents a cure for AIDS. But when you consider the potential for life, the number of children people could have if they dedicated themselves to nothing else is stupendous. Think of all those possible Mozarts and cancer cures. That's the potential every healthy human possesses in their loin. Does this mean people have a moral obligation to have as many children as possible, or that they love life less because they choose to have only a few or no children? This life potential is plentiful not only in our own natures, but also via means of science. Suppose (hypothetically) some geek in a lab figures out how to genetically clone human embryos. The potential that exists there is no different than that which exists for any newly conceived child. Should that scientist then breed as many children as he can in order to release all that potential life? All that potential music and medicine?

For myself, when still so recent a conception as to be unaware of its physical self, then, though unfortunate, the termination of that embryo seems the same as choosing not to use that ever-present potential to create life. Like simple non-conception.

Perhaps the elusive concept of their own non-conception is what elicits some to oppose abortion. It may be just a tad disturbing for certain people to think about the fact that they themselves were biologically nothing more, nor less, than the union of one of many eggs and sperm. Or, in other words, your parents could *not* have had you just as easily or even easier than they *did* have you. Perhaps abortion bothers some people as much as it does because it makes them have to contemplate just how mortal, just how temporary and circumstantial all our lives here really are.

Who knows? Besides, who am I to explain the mindset of those who so passionately oppose abortion? The best I can do is make my own feelings on the issue clear as possible, that it is a sad and unfortunate murder to be sure, but as long as women want this operation they should have the legal right to it.

And I love and cherish life as much as anyone, as do most pro-choicers, I'm sure. I don't believe for a second (despite the repeated claims of Limbaugh—see below) that there is anyone who supports a woman's freedom of choice who similarly thinks that abortion is the *better* of the two choices (unless it's some population control fanatic)—what most of us believe is simply that a woman should be free to choose for herself which path she takes.

Limbaugh: "I'm not opposed to abortion because I want to force people to do things my way. . . ." No, his opposition is based instead on his love for life. I can believe that. But Limbaugh can in no way believe that for feminists it's an issue of individual rights. ". . . believe me, to them it is a question of power. It is their attempt to impose their will on the rest of society, particularly men." And he says that "abortion is the fuel running their entire political agenda. It is the sacrament of their religion of feminism. . . . [their] objective is to see that there are as many abortions as possible." Again Limbaugh trips up his own position by characterizing his opposition with the grimmest of fallacies.

Hey, I'm all in favor of encouraging women to bear their children. But, while I can appreciate the sentiment of the pro-life movement, often it seems that their approach is off-putting to the very women they're trying to "convert" to their view. It's easy to hold protests outside clinics harassing those who work and those who go for operations there. This is certainly easier than it is to rationally encourage women to give birth because it's what *they* want to do, not because it's what they're told they must do by the law or pro-lifers (or imaginary celestial beings).

On the other side of that, it'd be wrong to support the right to an abortion—not only their legality, but their affordability—and not equally support services that help mothers who decide they *do* want to bear their child, whether they decide to keep it themselves or put it up for adoption.

That's how I feel about abortion, roughly and in so many words.

THE MYTH OF
FAMILY VALUES

As defined by yours truly, a victim complex is when someone projects injustices of the past as insurmountable obstacles to success, so that ultimately what holds them back is the fallacies of their own mind. That certain people embrace this complex (to avoid confrontation with their own fears and insecurities; as an excuse to be lazy or to do bad things) is a given.

But the way Limbaugh talks—constantly bemoaning this complex as though it were an epidemic of Biblical proportions—you'd think self-pity and sloth were the sole reason anyone is poor. Crying foul this victimization excuse has become an excuse onto itself (sort of an excuse-excuse) Limbaugh uses to dismiss welfare and other forms of public assistance as enablers of poverty.

Limbaugh compares government welfare to a giant sow and compares poor people to *piglets*. "The poor in this country are the biggest piglets at the mother pig and her nipples. The poor feed off the largesse of this government and they give nothing back. Nothing. . . . They're the ones that are always pandered to." And he asks whether the poor "pay anything back? Do they pay any taxes? No. They don't pay a thing. They contribute nothing to this country. They do nothing but take from it."

In addition to portraying welfare recipients as lazy piglets who do nothing but take, take, take without ever giving anything in return—70% of recipients get off welfare within two years—Limbaugh also compares them to drug addicts. "Helping people to become self-sufficient is much more compassionate than drugging them with the narcotic of welfare." And who's the drug pusher? Why the evil liberals of course! Limbaugh accuses liberal leaders such as Jesse Jackson of encouraging the American people to "reduce ourselves to the lowest common denominator; to emulate the poor, rather than encourage them to emulate those who produce."

Limbaugh suggests the government's being sucked dry because liberals are encouraging *everybody* to become dependent on welfare. "We're getting to the point where the tax producers will someday be outnumbered by the tax eaters of society." And according to him: ". . . while the sow is large she is near death. She's not fat and flourishing, she's emaciated."

And once the liberals fulfill their Utopia of getting everybody hooked on welfare, there will be no more taxpayers to provide for the giant sow, and then the government and our society will self-destruct. That's a logical scenario, huh? Sheesh, for someone who ridicules scientists for their doom and gloom hysterics (*about things like the cholesterol content of movie theater popcorn!*), Limbaugh certainly doesn't hesitate to present doomsday-like scenarios of how welfare's gonna bring down America.

Just about all I can think of to explain the attitude of those fundamentally opposed to welfare is an attachment to romantic notions of our past. This is certainly evident in Limbaugh's repetitious tendency—usually when decrying the heinous "welfare state"—of singing flowery, near-saccharine praises of how our noble forefathers founded this country out of a rugged work ethic. (Funny how Limbaugh so romanticizes our forebear's struggles, as if, had he lived in those times, his behemoth behind would have been trailblazing across the unsettled plain. It'd certainly have given new meaning to "where the buffalo roam.") Another of his 'Undeniable Truths' is that, "There is a distinct singular American culture—rugged individualism and self-reliance—which made America great." And he says we need to "wean people off the government pig. The country is losing its self-reliance and becoming a subsidy hog."

There's no denying that hard work is the main key to success in life, but what about those for whom harsh circumstance has put them in dire straits? What about those who could use a life preserver in today's sink-or-swim society?

The immediate past most likely was a simpler and more pleasant time in which to live, back when it was still reasonable to just stake some land, grow your own eats and live a relatively simple existence raising a family. Were it an option, surely many people would prefer to live back before this country became paved, before all this technology erupted and complicated everything. But there is no denying this technology—you'd think someone who met his third wife on Compu-Serve (like Limbaugh did) might recognize this—or how hectic all this change has made modern survival.

In the wake of these changes, it'd be awfully irresponsible not to have public programs to help those drowning from circumstance, teaching those unlucky few to swim these sudden high tides.

ILL LEGIT

Who exactly are these vermin-like poor Limbaugh claims is sucking the government dry? The sick, the elderly, and women are the lazy piglets to whom Limbaugh refers, and most of them women with children. And who arguably could be in greater need of financial assistance than a woman raising children all by her lonesome?

But Limbaugh argues that child subsidization and welfare *encourages* illegitimacy. ". . . the federal government has replaced the wage-earning husband and father with a welfare check. The man is no longer essential for financial support. Welfare . . . has emasculated John Q. Stud. He has reverted to irresponsibility." But by saying such, Limbaugh contradicts his own ideals of individual responsibility. It is *he* who is shifting responsibility *away* from the individual by claiming John Q. Stud acts irresponsibly because of welfare. These men don't do this because of the government, they do it because they're heartless scum who care about no one but themselves—and you'd better believe they're going to feel this way welfare or no welfare. These pricks are responsible for their own selfish behavior, and to suggest their immoral actions are simply a response to this government program is to soften the blunt of responsibility such scoundrels must be forced to bear.

But Limbaugh suggests that if welfare didn't exist, then these fathers would act responsibly and support their children. "We must quit rewarding fathers for leaving their families and mothers for having more kids out of wedlock. We must remove government as the father figure support base in these inner city families and provide incentives for the real fathers to stay home." I wasn't aware that most people's sense of responsibility in life was shaped by the government. And I've always been under the impression that for anyone with *any* sense of responsibility whatsoever, the incentive to "stay home" was to provide for the ones you love and care about. Is Limbaugh honestly going to have us believe that a father's sense of love and responsibility for his children is dictated by welfare, what he refers to as a *giant bloated pig*?

An elaboration of this anti-welfare sentiment can be found in a *Wall Street Journal* article entitled "Tomorrow's Underclass," in which one Charles Murray says, "... society's signal to a single woman should be unmistakable: to have a baby that you cannot care for is irresponsible, and the government will no longer subsidize it." He further states that: "We must make marriage once again the sole legal institution for parental rights and responsibilities." What he means, as best as I can figure, is that it must be made clear that if women expect any help raising their children, then they must be married, and that any children they have out of wedlock will solely be their own financial burden.

Anti-welfare conservatives, though they believe they are, aren't truly trying to end illegitimacy. If they were they might recognize that the real blame belongs to the fathers, not the women they abandon. Rather, they're trying to end single parenthood by placing all the blame on the mothers.

Their underlying message is eons old traditionally: men aren't responsible for sticking their dick in a vagina, and women are strictly responsible for any child that comes out of it. That since women bear and usually feel the greatest sense of nurturing for children, they are consequently responsible not only for their own egg but also the sperm that fertilized it, while men don't even have to take responsibility for their own love-gunk. (But by making all parents financially accountable for their offspring without the necessity of a marriage license, then maybe this will discourage the true causers of illegitimacy from being so irresponsible for the children they help spawn.)

The men who leave are the irresponsible ones. The women, on the other hand, *are* being responsible—they're sticking it out, trying to do the right thing, trying to raise their children. But Limbaugh wants people to believe that these women are nothing but "a bunch of fat piglets" who "feed off the largesse of this government and . . . give nothing back" because all they do is "sit around basking in self-pity."

Now isn't that right Rush?

MURPHY BROWN: ANTICHRIST

Fear of financial loss is the only practical way for our government to help prevent illegitimacy. What else can be done? Preach: "Family values, family values—that's the answer to all our problems. Happy thoughts and family values!"? Or maybe force everyone to watch reruns of *Ozzie and Harriet* and *Father Knows Best*—strap everyone into chairs and pry their eyelids open. That'd fix everything, huh?

For quite some time now, from around when Dan Quayle made his infamous *Murphy Brown* speech, I've been trying to figure out just what exactly "family values" is supposed to mean. Hey, don't get me wrong, I love and value my family as much as the next fella, but in no way do I believe this means I have *family values*. I'm still mostly unclear on the matter, but to the best of my knowledge family values is a mythical term meant to recall the artificially-produced halcyon days of the 50's nuclear family. And, to a large degree, this myth is utilized to justify attacks against such sinister threats to the family system as single parents and welfare.

Either that or family values is nothing more than a Christian term for in-home Bible studies. If the lacking of this is what's causing the decline of our nation, then may anarchy rule!

Limbaugh tells us that: "The real message of that *Murphy Brown* episode was that . . . total fulfillment and happiness can be achieved without men or husbands." If showing a single mother on TV is tantamount to an attack against men and husbands, then isn't showing two parents on TV tantamount to an attack against single parents? Well then, as someone raised by a single mom, I must call for an immediate boycott of these hateful shows.

This exaggeration is meant to illustrate how Limbaugh is an extremist in the truest sense. Meaning that not only does he hold extreme views, but through his eyes everything in opposition to his steadfast beliefs is equally extremist. He's so fanatical in his belief that the ideal two parent household is the *only* acceptable norm that to him a television show which depicts a *successful* single mother is presenting an equally extremist and fanatical view that ". . . women don't need men [and] shouldn't desire them. . . ." Notice I emphasized *successful*, for I honestly don't believe had Murphy Brown been depicted as a crackhead single mother on welfare that Limbaugh would have criticized the show . . . if anything, he'd laud it for illuminating the evils of single parenthood.

What makes people believe that a child raised by one parent will become a little delinquent, but with two parents they're sure to become an upstanding citizen? One good parent is a hell of a lot better than two lackluster ones. Believe it or not, my mom raised *four* children almost completely by herself to, by most standards, excellent success, and she never preached the Ten Commandments or subjected us to any other "family values" either.

The benefit of having two parents, besides the financial support, is simply that the mathematical odds for having good parents is increased with the increased number of parental units; it's not a guarantee of anything, though, nor a reason to stigmatize single parents. I mean, just imagine how much higher the probability for raising a well-adjusted child might be with three or four parents—would that then be a reason to attack two parent households?

The issue here is *poor parenting*, something which reaches across all households no matter how many parents are present, and it is this that should be the main focus of our attention in this nation's ever-increasing problem of violent, out-of-control kids. But I can't even begin to talk about what it takes to be a good parent. Not only because I have no children of my own but because I do know this much: a person is only as good a parent as they are a person in general. Meaning parenting is a reflection of who someone is as a person, and the quality of their parenting can only be as good as they are an individual. This isn't to imply the less educated are more likely to be bad parents; the ability to love and nurture, that which is most essential, is one which too reaches across all households. But also do the sensibility of the parent's beliefs and attitudes toward life play an enormous role in shaping their child's psyche. And as perhaps I've demonstrated herein, one's beliefs and attitudes can be a somewhat complex matter.

AMERICAN JUSTICE:

PUNISHMENT

vs

REHABILITATION

So as to better illustrate my position, I'll be making reference to an incident which occurred over four years ago. But whether it occurred yesterday or before Christ, it remains a perfectly suitable example of how, when it comes to criminal justice, most people tend to let their worst emotions rule.

The incident to which I refer is when, not too long ago, an American named Michael Fay was sentenced in Singapore to receive six lashes (reduced to four thanks to pressure from the U.S.) to his rear end. The skin of the offending buttocks is split open on the first lick, and it only gets worse after that. The medical community compared this to the equivalent of torture. Yet to my astonishment people across our entire country, even people I knew personally, applauded this punishment as just and proper. And so naturally I was curious as to what Limbaugh had to say about it, mostly because of his tremendous weight . . . with the American people.

And oddly enough, somehow I actually thought he might condemn the lashing. Go figure. Not that I was *surprised* when he didn't condemn it (I'd come to the point where only the most vile of idiocy to spew from his large head could surprise me), but I *was* disappointed. He sat there and not only didn't condemn it, but suggested we should be learning from Singapore's punishment system. "There's a lesson to be learned from the way Singapore is running its affairs. We ought to learn it and learn it fast."

I was under the impression that the fundamental premise on which America was founded was freedom. And that this included the freedom of all citizens, even those who *have* broken the law, not to be subjected to cruel or unusual punishment.

No doubt if we ran our affairs like Singapore there'd be less crime. For instance, if, like the Singapore government, we had no due process and the courts didn't care whether there was any reasonable doubt about the guilt of the accused, and if drug dealers were all executed, and if the government came up with a lot of arbitrary laws like banning chewing gum and fining people for not flushing public toilets, and if surveillance cameras were put in all public places, then surely the crime rate here in the States would drop dramatically. But at what a terrible cost.

A high crime rate is a small price to pay for the incredible freedom we're allotted in this country, and I wouldn't give it up for all the sterile security in Singapore.

TWO WRONGS

Limbaugh is quite fond of calling into question other people's true intentions on any number of issues. Animal rights activists are only out to devalue human life; environmentalists are only out to punish the American way of life; abortion rights activists want to see as many abortions occur as possible in order to have power over men; homeless advocates actually want people to remain homeless so they can keep a stranglehold on their lucrative Poverty Industry. And of course the elitist liberals want to do all the above. Even when he's willing to admit these people's actions may be inspired by compassion, Limbaugh still manages to attribute some deranged motivation to their compassion. "These people Care. . . ." Rush tells us. "They care so much that caring becomes a crutch that makes them feel special and more noble than the rest of us." Ironically nobody seems to Care about victims of crime more than conservatives like Rush. They care so incredibly much they want the victimizers tortured for their crimes. Now that's *true* compassion! Uh-huh.

Clearly the intent of these punishments is to instill respect through fear. But fear isn't respect. Fear doesn't earn one's respect. Respect is understanding, admiration, love. Fear is fear. It is an intensely foul feeling that goes against one's grain, disturbs and disrupts the soul, one's mental well being.

Most people coming out of prison are already filled with a fair amount of resentment. Can you imagine how they'd feel if the prisons were made even *more* horrible, into torture camps (to deter them no less!)? Unless they actually brainwash criminals like they did in *A Clockwork Orange* or in *1984*, or the torture leaves them broken spirited (in which most cases I'd assume after parole they'd end up homeless or in mental institutions for the rest of their crime-free lives), this approach to criminal "deterrence" is seriously bent. Rather than turning them into law-abiding Samaritans, it'd probably have the opposite effect in that many convicts would cross a mental breaking point where they'd simply stop caring for their own lives, they'd feel desperate and suicidal. No one is more dangerous to a free society than a criminal with no sense of value for their own life, nothing to lose.

Limbaugh has his own provocative thoughts on criminal justice: "There's a simple way to solve the crime problem: obey the law; punish those who do not." Food for thought indeed. He believes prisons have forgotten the value of punishment (what with these pansy liberals being lenient on everyone for their crimes), and, in addition to condoning Singapore's torture methods, has said that if prisons were all hard labor camps out in the middle of the burning hot desert, then surely convicts would never again break the law.

But how can the system expect to take someone whose mindset is already halfway to hell—metaphorically speaking—and take them all the way down that pit and expect it to correct them, expect one act of evil to cancel out another? Two wrongs do not a right make. You cannot torture a tortured soul and expect it to cure them. The only way to truly deter anyone from anything is by showing them a better way.

Good parenting is a deterrent. A good education is a deterrent. The law and law enforcement, security alarms, steel bars across your windows, and a moat are all perfectly good deterrents. Simply catching a criminal and isolating them from our society is a deterrent. But a criminal's body does not react on its own, all their actions flow from their mind. So whereas they can commit physical crimes and can be physically deterred from this (incarceration, torture, death), it is their criminal *minds* that must be amended.

That doesn't mean giving them electric shock or lobotomies, either. There's no specific criminal brain matter you can scoop out. Nor is a criminal filled with demons you can exorcise by thrashing them like a carpet full of dust. You cannot correct a criminal by treating their physical self, for it is their, and our and everyone's mental, intangible self that runs the show.

ANONYMOUS NO MORE

Prisons clearly shouldn't be places of torture (at least in my "left-wing radical" opinion) . . . but neither should the prisoners be spoiled. And though even under the best of circumstances incarceration is surely no amusement park, numerous prisons are loaded up with all sorts of creature comforts, luxuries, and recreational activities, ordered by state courts under the banner of "rehabilitation."

Let's be clear about what rehabilitation constitutes. It is not a once-a-week therapy session that's automatically gonna cure convicts of their criminal instincts, nor is it a lot of side programs existing separately from the formal prison environment. It's *everything* they do in prison, from the moment they awake to when they go back to bed, and it needs to be intense. What else are they there for? To whittle the days of their sentence away lifting weights and learning how to become better criminals?

And do understand, when I say rehabilitation needs to be *intense*, I'm not talking about making the inmates miserable. They can easily be made to suffer, but this isn't going to bring about any epiphany that: the place they're in makes them miserable, they're in this place because of their crime, and therefore they'll never repeat such acts. Yeah—think again. Yet this must be the faulty logic made by those people who think prison should be a torturous place. If inmates are made miserable in such a way, the most they'll feel for their crime is sorry that they were *caught* doing it, not sorry that they actually *did* it.

The prison environment shouldn't be purposely cruel, but neither should it allow inmates such diversions that they may forget why they are even in prison. Inmates should never be allowed to forget why they're inside, especially when they first enter—not necessarily because they broke the law, disturbed and disrupted the peace, or violated someone else's rights, but because of their specific crimes.

Coming to grips with their exact criminal activity, all of its ramifications and consequences, is the starting place from which a criminal may begin to see their behavior in a more harsh and revealing light. Of some importance to this process is getting the criminal's victims and all people affected by what they did involved with their rehabilitation (at their own disclosure, of course).

Twisted as this sounds, it might be pretty eye-opening for criminals and their victims to, in a controlled, safe environment, meet each other face to face. Talk to one another on a human level. Let the criminal see the face of the person or people they've hurt, look into their eyes. For the criminal it's often a faceless "victim," not a real person. The anonymity of their victims coupled with an ignorance of the real-life consequences of their actions makes it that much easier for criminals not to take their offenses seriously or understand why what they did was reprehensible and regrettable. (See Appendix VI for a random thought on rehabilitation.)

STRIFE AFTER DEATH

INTRODUCTION

You'll notice this is another of those chapters (like so many before it and more yet to come) that has more of a subsequent relation to Limbaugh than a direct one. That's because, based on what I've heard on his show and read in his first book, his position doesn't lend itself well to any kind of real debate. He supports the death penalty basically because it's the will of the majority of people and because criminals must know there are consequences to their actions. But simply by virtue of his position, however poorly justified, what follows certainly points directly to why his position is wrong.

Deterrence is the act of protecting one's self and/or protecting others from dangerous individuals, and it takes place in the streets and wilds of our world—once in custody, however, criminals are not a direct threat to society and anything purposely bad done to them is an unnecessary abuse of power.

Not that this has stopped our so-called *intelligent* and *civilized* species from endlessly finding ways to justify our bloodlust in the name of the larger good. The reason, or rather excuse, most often given by government officials for the death penalty is as a deterrent against crime and violence. But the death penalty's only practical function is as a PR tool, something politicians can use to fool citizens into believing that justice is being served and crime being deterred. It's the equivalent of Romans throwing Christians and other "undesirables" to the lions, and about as meaningful.

California Governor Pete Wilson: "Killers have no place in the civilized society of California. . . . I will do everything in my power to see to it that the people of California remain protected by the death penalty." Is that why we're gonna kill them, because they don't belong in our 'civilized society'? Isn't that what prisons are for, to detain those deviants who do not belong in our society?

It's often said that this protects us directly from the person being murdered (such as in Pete Wilson's aforementioned assurance), but sometimes it's also implied that this subsequently deters people on the street from committing crime.

But how could it be a deterrent? The very people it's meant to deter are committing crimes so heinous, it's not logical to assume that they value their own life so much as to be discouraged by the threat of "capital punishment." There's not a shred of evidence to indicate that America's death penalty has *ever* had a direct or subsequent impact on lowering crime or homicide anywhere it's been implemented.

Limbaugh counters such statements by saying that the only way we'll ever find out whether this punishment has a deterring effect is for us to *use it*. But our government's been killing criminals since its founding and there's absolutely no indication in our society that this is deterring crime or violence. What makes him believe the continued use of the death penalty will reap different results?

It's clear to myself, at least, that the death penalty's real purpose is to satisfy the fear and neurosis of a people who're fed up with this senseless violence and feel helpless before this problem. Everyone wants to see crime deterred, but how? In the face of digging for deeper answers, people choose to express this confusion through an equally senseless act of violence. The only purpose of the death penalty is to provide people with a false sense of order, a false sense of power, and most definitely a false sense of justice.

INSTITUTIONALIZED

People argue that killing killers *is* justice, or "an eye for an eye." And yet murderers are the only criminals we extend this philosophy towards anymore; probably the only ones we would continue to view as *acceptable.* Someone who's convicted of shooting but not killing another isn't shot in the same fashion. A person convicted of cutting another with a knife isn't given the same wounds. You couldn't bloody well rob a thief, per say, but you could cut off his hands. Rapists aren't purposely raped and child molesters aren't purposely molested; course you can guess for yourself what would *actually* be done to those convicted of sex crimes.

On principle alone you'd think people would be suspect of a government that, by committing acts of coldblooded murder, is breaking, holding itself above, and superseding the laws it holds all citizens to. I suppose people feel this is alright so long as it's *legally* premeditated, wrapped up in red-tape and bureaucracy: institutionalized murder.

Which is likely the reason quite a few media folk would like to televise these executions—granted some would televise it just for the ratings, but for many it's a matter of public record, the citizen's right to know exactly what happens within our own government. These things weren't always done in such low-key or secretive ways. Used to be that these executions were done in public, often in the form of hangings or far more cruel devices of death. Nowadays, though, it's hidden from the public, and is being done in cleaner and more "humane" ways.

Judge Marilyn Hall Patel of San Francisco recently ruled that California's state gas chamber is unconstitutional under the 8th Amendment as it's "cruel and unusual punishment." In his statement the judge wrote that, "Our society no longer considers lethal gas an acceptable means by which to execute a person . . . [it] has no place in civilized society."

As if there *were* an acceptable means of execution in a 'civilized' society, or a cruelless form of murder. It's a complete contradiction, more literal than that oxymoron "government intelligence." That our society still believes there *is* an acceptable means of execution and that this protects us or is a form of justice only goes to demonstrate just how uncivilized we remain.

Myself, I've felt radically different about the death penalty over the years. At times I wasn't sure how I felt, and during others I *was* for it. Not because it meant anything to me but because I didn't care and figured, "Go ahead and kill 'em, what difference does it make to me?" Sometime since then I've given it more thought and have found that the death penalty does in fact sicken me. But that's basically the depth of the reason given by most people I know who support this punishment. It's always in some detached, bullshitting sort of way, like, "Screw it, who cares? Fry the guy." The perfect image I see is of Beavis (or was it Butthead?) chanting to the television: "Give him the chair! Give him the chair! Huh, huh."

The death penalty has been sanitized, cleaned up and hidden so it won't weigh on the public conscious (much like the Nazis hid their evil deeds from the innocent but knowing eyes of their pure Aryan people) and nobody will have to think about it on any other level than as a concept somewhere in the back of the mind. The state does much as it can nowadays to allow citizens to endorse this without ever having to actually witness what it is they've endorsed, without feeling that any of the blood is on their own hands.

And were these murders televised, many people's blind beliefs would be shattered under the gruesome image of the taking of a real human life. (Although I have no doubt quite a few people would also sit there guzzling their beer and rooting for the execution like they do their favorite football team.)

WHEN MEMORIES ARE ALL THAT REMAIN

Everyone must mourn for a loved one who has died, and I certainly can't expect people to just forgive and/or forget the fiend who may have taken a loved one's life. But by allowing vengeance toward the victimizer to consume them, aren't people doing the greatest harm to the memory and spirit of the victim?

Limbaugh asserts that people who oppose capital punishment care more about the rights of criminals than the rights of their victims. We're told by proponents that the execution of a murderer puts members of the victim's family at ease. But I wonder just how helpful it really is. It does nothing to bring back their loved one. And such a heady vengeance must leave an indelible impression that's next-to-impossible to separate from memories of their loved one. And when all that remains are one's memories, I'd think the most important thing to do after such a tragedy occurs is to preserve the memory of their dearly departed in as pure and undistorted a light as possible. Can this be accomplished when the last significant act done in their name, in their spirit, is to murder he who murdered them?

Those suffering such a loss must ask themselves: Is that honestly what their loved one would want, was that the content of their heart, that they would want their victimizer brutalized in return?

Nothing can be done to reverse the physical murder of a loved one, but people can still do something for themselves by not allowing the villain to also stain that loved ones memory, which lives on with those who were closest to them. That is the secondary tragedy of such horrors, that which people *can* prevent but don't. Hate is the easiest outlet of such strong emotions of pain, loss and grief, and consequently the least healing or productive, and the most personally disturbing and unsettling.

UBIQUITOUS
BOY TOYS

Freedom being the foundation upon which America began, surely when the constitution was written it was proper and prudent to allow citizens the unregulated ownership of firearms. But, in light of all the changes that have coming crashing over our nation like a tidal wave, specifically our advancements in weapons technology, how can such a haphazard legality continue to be the national standard?

It's common knowledge that man is dangerous. It's dizzily optimistic to think you can allow everyone access to the most powerful firearms available without this creating some ugly problems in return. Especially when you have an intense crime-fueling element like drugs booming in poverty-stricken inner cities.

But instead of being willing to engage in intelligible discourse on the moderation of gun ownership, the National Rifle Association is fundamentally (and some might say zealously) opposed to *any* restrictions made against the right to bear arms, citing the infallibility of the 2nd Amendment.

Never mind that instead of the single shot muskets they had back then, today's guns are capable of successive rapid-fire discharge. Never mind that instead of the riders of Pony Express times, today's disgruntled postal worker is packing Uzis and Ak-47s. Never mind that back when this country was founded, a kid who wanted to play with their dad's gun had to first load it with gunpowder and ammo, whereas all kids today have to do is look in the closet or the dresser by the bed. Never mind the far more complicated and delicate nature of today's social troubles. The NRA is willing to ignore all these realities in favor of their armed-to-the-teeth Utopia.

Given how insistent NRA members are to defend the 2nd Amendment above all other considerations, and given their penchant for owning the most powerful of weaponry, a firearm novice such as myself can't help but wonder how many gun enthusiasts are simply sportsmen, and how many aren't perhaps trying to *compensate* for some other *shortcoming*.

And then some enthusiasts are just hard-core paranoid. There are many so-called patriots who believe America is a law away from becoming a fascist dictatorship (usually under control of the nefarious U.N.), and that the only way to guarantee our freedom is for everyone to own as many firearms as possible. They crave the oh-so-sweet assurance of feeling they can be safe from all life's evils so long as they've got their trusty assault rifle (or Bible, for that blasphemous matter) to hold and protect them.

I'm unaware as to whether Limbaugh is himself a member of the NRA, but whatever the case his views clearly fall in line with that all-or-nothing extremism. Limbaugh has said that Americans need the 2nd Amendment, specifically interpreted as the *unlimited* right to bear arms, in order to protect the 1st Amendment. As if to imply that without these assault and automatic weapons at our disposal, the government would quickly forbid freedom of religion and of the press. There are more practical ways to keep our government in check, such built-in safeguards as a balance of powers, publicly elected officials, constituency, etcetera.

I am quite aware that the majority of gun enthusiasts aren't in the mind of robbing or killing other humans. But still, all a gun is is a toy, a real deadly and destructive one. It is also a tool of power, of control, and I can certainly understand why people would be concerned about a government that exclusively held this power over its citizens. But only a hard-line radical would argue that people shouldn't be allowed to own *any* firearms—all I'm saying is that it should be done in a reasonable manner, not with reckless abandon to insure that people can overthrow the government! (I think the idea is to allow people ownership of that which can be used effectively for sport or safety, but not allow ownership of firearms so powerful that, if in the wrong hands, could easily be used to slaughter a great deal of people in a short amount of time.)

MOSES MY ASS

Limbaugh complains that Hollywood isn't glamorous like it was back in its heyday, whenever that was exactly. You've got these trouble-making directors like Spike Lee and Oliver Stone putting all their emphasis on the negative of our distinguishable past, you've got idiot filmmakers making t&a gorefests when clearly *Bambi* is all anyone ever wants to see. And you've got a lot of clueless movie stars inappropriately using their celebrity to champion "leftist" causes such as the environment and homelessness.

But apparently Limbaugh only has a problem with the latter if he disagrees with the celebrity's cause. Talk about movie stars using their celebrity to endorse ridiculous things—how about Charlton Heston supporting the NRA's protest of the president's proposed ban on assault weapons? Yet despite his annoyance with these other celebrity activists, Limbaugh roundly applauded Heston for his gesture.

During a press conference, Mr. Heston held up a picture of some guy that'd killed a bunch of people (I wasn't familiar with the man or his crimes) with "This is an assault weapon" → pointing at the man. Undoubtedly serial killers would persist without guns (it never stopped psychos like Jack the Ripper, Ed Gein, or Ted Bundy) and people will still be killed. But tell the people who were on that Long Island Railway that. Or those people in that SoCal McDonalds or that Luby's Cafeteria in Texas. Or all those postal workers.

Keeping heavier artillery out of the hands of the general public isn't going to end crime or violence, but, in specific instances and to the benefit of many lives, it certainly might help slow it down to a more survivable level.

PRIORITIES

Most people take for granted the meaning of freedom, when actually it is open to varied interpretation—at least in the contexts of a government. For in the absolute sense, freedom means being able to kill and rape and pillage without any laws whatsoever.

But in the context of a government whose purpose is to help protect its citizens, freedom means something quite different; it means restricting certain freedoms in order to protect other more treasured and valued freedoms. That's the paradox of freedom through government—you can't *have* any freedom without the sacrifice of freedom. In that respect freedom *isn't* free; I don't think it should cost someone their life (such as in a military draft), but it definitely requires some sacrifices in return.

Obviously the most significant "sacrifice" made is in our right to endanger the well being of others. And the consequences of people's actions is directly related to what they are allowed to own. If people were allowed ownership of nuclear weapons, for instance, then the detonation of such a device in the owner's home would most certainly infringe upon the freedoms of his neighbors—and so, despite those mental cases who might argue that bombs don't kill people, people kill people, this worst-case scenario clearly demonstrates the necessity of restricting what citizens are allowed to own.

Much more than protecting people from the cruelty or carelessness of others, though, the state also extends this to protect those people who might harm themselves with the use of controlled substances. (But again, you hear very few individuals defending cocaine or heroin chanting, "Drugs don't kill people, people kill, um, themselves . . . or something.") Like guns, drugs *don't* kill people. Such substances are simply the dangerous vehicle by which people kill themselves, and for that reason alone they should be illegal. To protect those people who might use, not own but *use*, certain drugs to their own endangerment.

And somehow it seems inconsistent and more than a little hypocritical that the same consideration of safety extended to people who might harm themselves (with the imprudent use of drugs) isn't extended just as—or even more seriously—to those who might harm others (with the negligent or naughty use of firearms). Do people really pose greater threats to themselves than they do to each other? It makes about as much sense as sending someone who attempts suicide to the electric chair while letting an attempted murderer off scot-free.

The parallels between drugs and guns run deep. There's the obvious correlation between drug prohibition and violent crime. There's the hypocrisy of a government more concerned for the well being of those who might knowingly harm themselves with drugs than for the innocent victims of shootings. And finally there's the contrast between drug laws sweepingly restricting drugs as if they were all alike; and gun laws sweepingly allowing firearms as if they were all alike. And much like my defense of recreational drugs, I feel similar about the relative safety of certain guns. But under our law a joint is considered more dangerous than an assault weapon. Talk about our priorities being out of whack! It should by now be fairly obvious where this analogy is headed, but I'll go ahead and spell it out for you anyway: Marijuana should be legal the same as sport and safety firearms—and narcotics and stimulants illegal the same as hard artillery. Much like hard drugs, certain guns should be restricted from the public—not because there's any danger in their ownership, but in their misuse; they should be prohibited because they are the dangerous vehicle by which so many people's lives are tragically ended.

REALISTIC REQUISITES

Think about what is required to drive a *car* on the streets of America. First you've gotta take driver's ed, which mainly entails reading a bunch of instructional manuals and watching gruesome films of real-life auto fatalities (presumably to hammer home just how serious a responsibility driving is, though it's more likely just to scare potential speeders and drunk drivers). Once you've passed driver's ed you get your driving permit. Then you've gotta take driver's training, only after so many hours of which you're allowed to take a written exam and a driving test to get your license. It's a fairly long and labored process meant to slowly educate one as to the nuances of safe driving. That's because a car in the hands of an inexperienced driver can be quite a dangerous thing; and yet despite all these safety precautions, look at how many idiot drivers there are out there! (Granted I live in Los Angeles, but I cannot believe these people's reckless driving habits are limited exclusively to the West Coast.)

In contrast to what it takes merely to drive an automobile, to buy a firearm all one need do is walk into any old gun store or corner pawnshop. To legally own that gun all one need do is register it. Now think of all those half-witted drivers out there—and yet surely a gun in the hands of an idiot or a lunatic can be infinitely more dangerous than the largest of automobiles driven by the elderliest of little old ladies. At the least owning a gun should require a safety course and a gun license much like that for driving a car. (Though frankly it's pretty scary to think of a bunch of militia members waiting to register their firearms in as frustrating a place as the DMV.)

I'm sorry if the idea of a requisite safety course and gun license sounds rash and Big Brotherish, but it's time to recognize firearms for the powerful tools of death and destruction they are, and that if our government is going to allow its citizens ownership of these, then it must be done so with much care and caution.

STEPPING OVER
A STEPPING STONE

Affirmative action, contrary to the apparent beliefs of some, was never intended as a means for enforcing or upholding civil rights against job discrimination. Limbaugh says, "Even if we get rid of affirmative action, there are anti-discrimination laws on the books. . . ." But if there were in fact a reliable way of detecting discimination in the workplace, then something like affirmative action never likely would have been necessary to begin with. Because, absent their wearing a pointy white sheet or having a swastika tattooed on their forehead, it's not real easy to prove that an employers hiring practices are based on race or sex as opposed to qualifications. There never likely will be a practical way of detecting or preventing most acts of hiring discrimination. The only realistic way for the government to counter widespread discrimination is by issuing hiring quotas.

More than anything I believe affirmative action was our government's way of making much faster inroads into the American economy for women and minorities than ever could have been accomplished were this to take place in its own natural time. Taking into account the sorry state of our racial and gender affairs as a result of hundreds of years of intense prejudice, this certainly was a positive thing to have been put into effect. And though affirmative action cannot be solely credited for the progress made in the last few decades, it was undeniably helpful in opening doors of social acceptance for a great many women, Latinos, African and Asian Americans.

Of course, *ideally* businesses should be left alone to do their own thing, independent of any government interference in who they do or do not hire. But then, in an *ideal* world the government never would have allowed white men to enslave and repress others to begin with. There's simply no denying the harm our government's apathy helped perpetuate against women and minorities; is it so much to ask that the same government finally try to make amends?

Affirmative action is undeniably a form of reverse-discrimination in that it passes over qualified Caucasian applicants simply on the merit of their race. But it is not a discrimination based on intolerance or the desire to hold another down; instead it is favoritism based on the desire to help right a heinous wrong, to economically assist those who for so long *have* been held down.

The problem is that in the conception of affirmative action, nobody appeared to think ahead as to what to do *when* progress is made and the playing field gradually becomes more leveled. Affirmative action surely was never intended as a permanent solution, but a temporary stepping stone. Well, we've reached a point now where it's necessary to recognize affirmative action as something that must soon end. This isn't to deny that much intolerance and prejudice still exists today; but the playing field, though hardly even, has leveled to such a point that workplace affirmative action seems more like the source for a poor self-image than that of economic beneficiary. Eventually all stepping stones must be put behind us if we're to make yet further progress.

But how exactly? *When* and *how* do we put affirmative action behind us? (The workplace aside, it might be a good idea if affirmative action were to continue for college scholarships. That may sound odd coming from a college dropout, but hey, I learned a lot in that first semester.) Probably most important is setting a specific date sometime in the near future so as to allow those people most impacted by affirmative action know it's going to end a fair amount of time beforehand. You can't blame people for having harsh reactions to this when it's done so spur-of-the-moment impulsively.

The real question then becomes that of getting our political representatives to either accept someone else's vision or come up with one of their own for how affirmative action can thoughtfully be phased out of existence.

That's the question. *That's* the issue.

BUNK THAT!

But Limbaugh says affirmative action must be stopped not only because it's a form of reverse-discrimination, but because race and sex are no longer relevant to one's success. On his radio show Limbaugh said, "I would like to, on this program, conduct a funeral for racism. 'Cause I think racism is not nearly as prevalent as everybody thinks that it is." He points out that, "Oprah Winfrey cannot become the richest and most popular, most watched daytime television talk show host with only black people in her audience." And rhetorically asks, "How in the world can Bill Cosby have become the number one television show without white viewers?"

Ah, there's that golden Limbaugh logic sputtering away again. Because of course if all these whiteys are supporting black entertainers, then surely racism is no longer a hindrance. By that same logic, if you look at how many white people were supportive of blacks during the Civil War, then surely racism couldn't have been all that bad way on back then. It's not like blacks could have been emancipated with only black people fighting the cause—indeed, they had enough white supporters that they were able to win a massive war. And in a time when so many white people were supportive of blacks (like they are today, as the Nielson ratings clearly indicate), by Limbaugh's logic one could then argue that racism was no longer a major issue during the most volatile of our nation's civil unrests.

To further illustrate the non-hindrance of one's race, Limbaugh mentioned the success of pop-star Michael Jackson, athletes Deion Sanders and Michael Jordan, and, his greatest examples, Gen. Colin Powell and Supreme Court Judge Clarence Thomas.

Surely the ability of minorities to rise to positions of prominence and power is greater than it's ever been; but speaking just in terms of accomplishment, if one is to point to the success of Thomas and Powell as proof that race is no longer relevant, couldn't one make a similar argument in reference to civil rights leader Booker T. Washington, scientist George Washington Carver, or sociologist Kelly Miller? Are we then to believe that racism was no longer relevant to the lives of African Americans back in the late 19th and early 20th century?

Prominent black Americans have existed throughout the history of our country and will continue and increase far into the future. Certainly there's far less oppression today, and the opportunity for minorities to succeed is greater than it's ever been. No one would deny that. But to claim this as proof for the *nonexistence* of discrimination, and to conclude that race and sex are no longer relevant, is absolutely asinine at best, a conscious lie at worst.

'Nuff said.

CONGRESSIONAL GANGRENE

As long as I'm already on the topic of workplace discrimination. . . . The favorite argument of people who are against homosexual anti-discrimination laws is that gays and lesbians shouldn't be given "special rights" based on their sexual preference. But are such anti-discrimination laws truly a special right so much as a basic civil right? How would such opponents feel if they were themselves turned down for a job they were perfectly qualified and capable of doing because, as the employer they were being interviewed by flat out told them, "We don't hire heterosexuals"? Would they view this in the same light they do homosexual discrimination?

During one of his daily news conferences in March '95, House Speaker Newt Gingrich disclosed his own disparaging feelings on the subject of gay rights. "I don't think you should have a right of filing a federal lawsuit or appealing to the federal government to protect you based on your sexual behavior."

To excuse why he feels homosexuals shouldn't have any legal recourse against hiring discrimination, Gingrich said something of the most inexplicable ignorance: "Does that mean a transvestite should automatically have the right to work as a transvestite? I don't think so." But homosexuality doesn't necessarily have a thing to do with being a transvestite. There are any number of transvestites who are heterosexual, guys with wives and kids who simply, for whatever reason, enjoy dressing in women's clothing.

The argument for giving homosexuals legal recourse against hiring discrimination isn't about allowing employees to behave or dress however they like. It's about the right to privacy; it's about people being fired for things they do on their own personal time which *in no way affects their job performance.*

For example: If a heterosexual female goes to work dressed like a ballerina, then that should give her employer all the right in the world to fire her ass (unless, of course, she's *actually* a ballerina); but they shouldn't have the right to fire her just because she's heterosexual. It should be the same for everyone: if an employee's personal life in no way interferes with their ability to perform their job, then their employer shouldn't have the right to fire them on the basis of this.

Why is that such a difficult concept to grasp?

The law states no one shall be discriminated against based on their race or gender, but nothing is mentioned about sexual preference. Why should it? A person's private life should remain just that, private.

That's exactly why we *do* need a law protecting people from discrimination based on their sexual preference, *to* protect a person's private life. Newt said, "I don't see as a general principle that getting into your private life is something we ought to have a legal standard on." What he once-again fails to comprehend is that so long as there is no law specifically meant to protect a person's private life from workplace discrimination, then this is essentially the same as *having* a legal standard that allows a person's private life to be the basis of such discrimination. Either because of a law or because of the absence of one, the government affects and gets into the private lives of anyone subject to unjust discrimination. I thought the whole purpose of legal standards was "getting into" people's lives, seeing to it that citizens and business owners don't have the right to use any possible power they may possess over another in a malicious or prejudice manner. You'd think the Speaker of the House of Representatives would understand a legal principle as rudimentary as that. (Then again, it *was* Gingrich who proclaimed Limbaugh an honorary member of the 104th Congress.)

"CHOOSING" THE HOMO "LIFESTYLE"

Gingrich further stated that America should not return to "repression" of gays and lesbians, but that neither should it "promote" a homosexual lifestyle. When did America ever stop its oppression of homosexuals? That's news to me!

What Mr. Gingrich fails to recognize is the fact that he himself *is* a repressor of homosexuals. He may like to believe that the only people who can be said to really repress homosexuals are skinhead Nazis who bash their skulls in, but the fact remains that the majority of gay and lesbian repressors has always been and continues to be people just like himself: uptight homophobic conservatives.

How does Gingrich think homosexuals are repressed—by burning them at the stake? Or by making them feel ashamed of who they are, afraid to disclose their homosexuality to anyone lest they should be ridiculed, rejected, or discriminated against?

By him saying that people shouldn't have any legal rights against hiring discrimination based on sexual preference, Gingrich *is* in effect repressing homosexuals. He wears his homophobia on his sleeve clear for all to see by accusing homosexual activists of "recruitment in so-called counseling programs," by warning against the idea of "explaining that homosexuality is a reasonable alternative lifestyle," and by saying that he is "very cautious about the idea that you want to have active homosexuals in junior high school and high school explaining to young people that they have all of these various wonderful options." He honestly seems to believe that to talk about homosexuality, to explain that it's not a mental sickness or disease or perversion, is to actively *encourage* kids to become homosexual. Almost as if he believes it's something you just choose to do one day. "Gee, I think I'll become a homosexual today . . . all my friends are doing it . . . seems like the 'cool' thing to do nowadays."

Gingrich is separating homosexuals from their homosexuality so that he can criticize and reject *it* while still believing he's not criticizing the people themselves. Why else would he refer to it as a "sexual *behavior*," as if it's simply something homosexuals chose to do or to become? That's almost like saying blacks shouldn't have any so-called *special rights* based on their "racial behavior." Or that women shouldn't have any rights based on their "gender behavior."

It's the exact same thing—it's who they are, not what they simply chose to become. Homosexuality isn't an act people *choose* to engage in any more than heterosexuality is an act people *choose* to engage in. Whether they're celibate their entire lives or not, a person is still either homo or hetero. A person's sexual orientation is ingrained within them and beyond their control as much as a person's race or gender.

DOWN AND OUT
IN AMERICA

When it comes to homelessness in America, Limbaugh has plenty to say about how liberals are just exploiting the issue to spurn class envy and make the middle class feel guilty. Limbaugh has lots to tell people about how the greatest obstacle to solving the homeless problem is that the liberal Poverty Pimps don't want the problem solved; how liberals are only interested in an ever-growing welfare state so they can keep all their friends employed. 'Cause, as he puts it, "Liberals can't stay in power if [the homeless] become self-sufficient."

The Fraud of Homelessness Advocacy, the name of a chapter in Limbaugh's first book, pretty clearly demonstrates where his priorities lie, focusing not on the homeless problem itself but on his pathetic anti-liberal fixation. Like many an issue, he has more to say about the follies of those actually looking to make a difference than he does anything constructive of his own to add.

"Real problems deserve real solutions, not name-calling." Or so concluded Limbaugh upon presenting his homeless solutions. Sure enough, after 12 pages of long-winded musings about the ulterior motives of wicked liberals; how Martin Sheen spent a night on the streets to bring attention to the issue; and how advocates like Mitch Snider exaggerated the number of homeless to be three million people, Limbaugh finally presented his "solutions" to the problem. A Five-Point Program. Which consisted of recommending, 1) getting an honest count of the homeless (which seemed strange seeing as how earlier in the chapter he said the number is probably close to the 600,000 given by the Urban Institute), 2) categorizing the homeless into their different needs, 3) getting those with addictions to alcohol or drugs into rehabilitation clinics, 4) putting the mentally ill or unbalanced into institutions, and, the cusp of his recommendations, 5) somehow (no specifics given) educating the able-bodied homeless "in how to access the boundless opportunities in the American economy."

Limbaugh says many homeless just aren't aware of the opportunities that are out there. I'd think only someone living on another planet would be unaware of the opportunities for employment that exist here in the States. The problem isn't that the homeless aren't aware of these opportunities, but that they don't know how or are unable to take advantage of them.

Having worked in a remedial paying profession for a few years now, I can tell you that whenever a homeless person came in to apply, they had absolutely no chance of getting the job; some of them because of their appearance, but all of them because they never left a telephone number or address.

Then the obvious answer to this would be to offer the homeless telephone services (a number they can receive messages on) and a legal address (maybe like a makeshift P.O. box system at shelters), as many businesses either won't or can't hire people without these. And by giving the homeless a telephone number and a legal mailing address, they might obtain a sense of connection with society—shit, I don't know! At the least they'd feel more confident in filling out job applications.

I'm not gonna claim to have any great ideas on how this problem can be solved, but certainly the homeless can't just be carted away to whatever facility might best be able to assist them. Someone's rights as an individual don't become null and void simply because they've no home to call their own. And so unless they're an immediate threat to others or themselves, I really don't see how there could be any legal basis for confining drug addicts or alcoholics to a rehabilitation clinic, nor the mentally unstable to institutions.

What the government *should* do to keep people off the streets is allow for squatter's rights. That the buildings people are squatting in are privately owned is immaterial—so long as the owners have clearly abandoned the buildings to just degenerate, there's no reason why the homeless shouldn't be allowed to take up residency within them. Naturally if an owner decides to rebuild, then their rights as a property owner would take precedence; but if the owner has abandoned their property, then, until such time as they decide to rebuild or pay for the demolition of the building, the rights of squatters to have a roof over their head should take full precedence.

HOMELESS HOT POTATO

Limbaugh's such a caring soul he recognizes that "liberals don't want the homeless to hold a job that has any real promise. They prefer to accommodate and humor them by making it easier for them to stay in their present condition. That's why they vigorously advocate a constitutional right to beg." Limbaugh's proposing that by allowing the homeless to panhandle liberals are only enabling their homelessness. He consequently seems to suggest that the outlawing of panhandling (not just aggressive, but all types) would be positive 'cause it'd *force* the homeless to straighten their lives out. Because of course were this right taken away they'd all get real jobs, since obviously the only thing that keeps them from doing so is the great satisfaction and wealth they must procure from begging for hand outs. (This train of logic serves well as another epitomes look into Limbaugh's thought-processes, and again it's rather disconcerting to say the least.)

Being that it's just a more direct form of charity—absent the middlemen—panhandling lies squarely in-between a life of crime and making an honest living; neither negative or positive, it is a fairly neutral source of income. Were this right taken away (as Limbaugh so compassionately suggested), then they pretty much *would* be forced to go either some negative or positive route. And is it truly reasonable to assume that, if forcibly pushed, most destitutes would be more inclined to go down a positive path, and be successful at it, than they would turning to a life of crime to fend for themselves?

I recall this one self-proclaimed "conservative" on *The Phil Dona-hue Show* (back in the day) saying how he has no sympathy for the homeless because it's so easy to get a job, how they're just lazy, and how he thought panhandling should be illegalized and the homeless arrested for loitering. When another person on the show asked him whether he honestly believed this approach did anything to solve the problem, the man was clearly befuddled for a second or two before answering that he thought it was important for the homeless to know what was *expected* of them by society.

Most must feel somewhat castoff already. Why then would they be eager to rejoin the very society that rejects and scorns them the second they're down on their luck? Why should the homeless, or *anyone* for that matter, give a rat's ass about what the "society" expects of them? (See Appendix VII for an arbitrary observation.)

Said approach of illegalizing panhandling and loitering is not to actually *illegalize* homelessness, but to put every law in the book possible to let them know they're unwanted, that their presence will not be tolerated. The only thing this satisfies is the public's desire not to have to see or deal with the homeless, lessening the burden of their conscious. It's like sweeping the problem under the rug, or more appropriately, it's sweeping it across the street. And of course once this problem builds up on the doorstep of another, they'll pass their own anti-homeless laws, passing the problem on to someone else.

Were this trend to catch on and escalate, it'd be like an endless game of homeless hot potato, shuffling them here and there like a herd of unwanted cattle.

The homeless problem cannot be solved by making the homeless so miserable that they're forced to either self-destruct or go straight. Discouraging homelessness solves nothing; the best anyone can do is to encourage others to pick themselves up *for themselves*—not the "society" or any other deranged reason—and of their own free will. Simply put: Those living on the streets must be discouraged from a life of crime; but still allowed the option of being homeless and of panhandling for a living; and they must be encouraged to help themselves.

CONCLUSION

A precise count of the homeless population may never exist, and nobody should need one to tell them there are too many without homes. Don't ignore these people. They have hearts and souls, dreams and goals (some realized, many forgotten), just like you and I. We're all so set in our routines, our fears, passing the homeless by like they're ghosts, not real people but simply a distasteful figment of the imagination. Granted some have serious mental problems and deserve to be feared—but usually this distance people put between themselves and the homeless isn't because of any real danger, but because people don't want to believe the same can happen to them, they fear seeing themselves in that person's tattered and torn shoes.

Hopefully more and more people will gradually overcome their irrational fear of the destitute (myself, to a fair degree or two, included), and will find the compassion to treat all other humans—no matter what their economic status—with the common kindness and respect they are deserving of.

LIKE, MAN,
WHO NEEDS A GOVERNMENT,
ANYWAY?

Americans *love* to bitch and moan about the government—not that there's anything intrinsically wrong with that, Lord knows there's plenty to bitch about. The soundness of people's grievance, however, varies considerably. Typically this is justified annoyance with the tax code and frustration with the Internal Revenue Service. But often this begrudgement is bred of a deeply embedded paranoia and fear of the government. There are Americans who talk so gravely of our state, they don't even seem to appreciate the fact that it's one of the great freedoms of that institution that allows them to openly denounce it.

Limbaugh got angry when, at a political debate between Ted Kennedy and Mit Romney, people asked what the candidates were going to do about crime. It *really* pissed Limbaugh off that all they wanted to talk about was issues rather than character, or as he put it: "What are you gonna give *me*, what are you gonna do for *me*?" He said these people need to stop whining, get off their butts, and do something about these problems themselves. Yeah, how right foolish of them: expecting the government, that shapes and enforces the law, to handle crime? What could have they have been thinking?! This, Rush said, was just another example of how all Democrats want is for the government to completely take care of everybody.

It's not easy explaining such irrational antigovernment sentiments, by Limbaugh or others. It must be strong religious attachments that causes certain people to so fear this other predominant institution; perhaps afraid of their religion being overshadowed or prohibited, which is understandable considering how many other governments around the world *do* infringe on their citizen's religious freedoms. But of course most people only have a problem with this if it's not *their* faith that's ruling. And so really it shouldn't be in the least surprising that there are people who have a problem with a government that neither condemns *nor* embraces any particular religion.

Human civilization can be foremost characterized as of a people interacting with one another in the contexts of self-imposed laws and commonly held standards. The most critical of such social structures have been religious and government institutions.

And though these are far from enlightening of themselves, they do help us to evolve in thought, providing us with a surface foundation from which to begin the learning process. In the chaotic abyss that is human consciousness, these structures supply an elemental sense of order and security from which people may go about the process of realizing guidance within themselves.

Unfortunately, the majority of these institutions have been less than accommodating towards individuality, based largely on conformist dogma. And unfortunately most of humanity has used these institutions as the basis for all their concepts of truth and identity altogether, in substitution of their own personal understanding.

But over time an increasing effort has been made to make the government more objective and religiously neutral (much to many believers great dismay). Even with the "separation of church and state," Americans continue to have a trying time grasping what that means, or how such concepts *are* kept separate.

Aside from the religious epithets still employed by our government, a good example of this is the continuing illegality of prostitution and, in certain states, sodomy. The laws illegalizing these are based on nothing more than certain people's religious beliefs. There is absolutely no sound basis for why such passive acts should be illegal. If a person chooses to sell their body for sex, or if a couple decides to engage in a little backdoor boogie, that should be no one's affair but their own. The only threat posed to anyone's freedom, in any sense, are those puritan-based laws that prohibit consenting adults from engaging in these sexual acts. This may not seem like a serious oppression to some, but it stands as a clear indicator of how we've yet to fully separate religion from state.

The government isn't meant to give guidance, to give people a sense of moral direction, nor should it be. The underlying purpose of any social structure should be to insure people's freedoms, which includes their physical and spiritual freedoms from oppression by others (the government itself most certainly included). Our government must work simply in terms of perceiving people's freedoms and then shaping the law so as to best protect these. It's freedom, not morality, that is the purpose of the government—the freedom by which people may realize their own sense of moral guidance.

Certainly this is the reason so many people are fearful of a godless government, because it allows more mental freedom than they're comfortable with. While a church-state encourages belief in that faith, and a Communist state encourages faith in the state, a government such as ours which has religious freedom seems to be saying that the truth doesn't lie in any of these faiths, but in all of them and none of them. Whatever works for each individual. Its neutrality seems like encouragement for everyone to search for their own beliefs. And what could be more frightening to a religious people who believe all truth lies in a single book?

Most ironic in describing our government's separation from religion is that, at the same time, it's developed its own rigid form of traditionalism. Of all the institutions that cling to the past, the government trails only slightly behind religion. But being that it's supposed to work for its citizens, the government isn't an institution quite like any other. It's much more like a business dealing in the assurance of freedom. And the only way for the vast majority of businesses to stay afloat nowadays is by trying their damnedest to stay one step behind, one step ahead, or in step with all the technological and cultural changes that have taken place.

And then politicians are perplexed as to why citizens are so displeased with the government? It's because they've failed, or rather resisted, to redesign their operations to accommodate the times; because they're practicing this prehistoric form of government in this rapidly changing, highly complex new world. The government's gotta come into the 21st century along with the rest of the country. Which means opening lines of communication and information; which means actually getting the job done as opposed to just taking comfort within the tradition of pomp and circumstance.

Another of the government's weaknesses is its deliberate over-complexity, otherwise known as bureaucracy. It was most likely a fear of using their great power in a negative manner that led our preceding politicians to create much of the bureaucracy that currently engulfs the government. Why? Trust, I'd assume, or a lack thereof—a lack of trust in their fellow man and possibly even in themselves, for, while their intent may have been genuine, perhaps they feared nonetheless using the enormous power of the government to great ill.

Today things *are* different, though. Oh sure, there are still religious fanatics who think America should be a church-state, there are still racists and sexists and all kinds of prejudiced people in this country, and the threat of the government to unfairly restrict the freedoms of its citizens always has been and always will be a matter of the utmost concern. But those safeguards no longer need be in the form of suffocating bureaucracy, as has been the case for far too long.

Limbaugh-like conservatives, on the other hand, seem to believe the main key to making our government more efficient is in blindly reducing its size and spending. And it seems to be in this insane vein that many politicians are campaigning to simply reduce the government, never mind actually *improve* how it works. It's the political equivalent of a bleeding, and should be about as effective as that practice was medically. (Don't you just love medieval medicine metaphors?)

The issue isn't how big the government is or how much it

spends—it's about *what* our government does and for *what* it spends our taxpayer money. Quality, not quantity, is what counts here. Clearly the quality of our government leaves much to be desired, but the solution isn't simply in declaring that it doesn't work because it's too big and spends too much money. Those are products of its inefficiency, not the cause of it.

The greatest and most obvious flaw of our government is the manner by which politicians are elected to office. Getting elected isn't cheap. It takes publicity, which doesn't come free. One must spend massive amounts of money to secure such positions. Which means raising the funds necessary to run for high political office opens the doorway to much corruption.

Money representing the special interest of certain organizations (like the NRA) or businesses (like the tobacco industry) in the form of campaign donations, gifts, or lobbyist junkets undoubtedly come with many strings attached, essentially making our highest elected officials prime targets for this bribery-like puppetry.

It's most vital that reform be made to the way campaign donations are given to political candidates. More than anything, it is this influence which taints the decisions made by certain representatives. It's really unbelievable how long such special-interest and corporate lobbying/campaign donations have gone unchallenged. Whose opinion do you suppose politicians value more—that of the people who vote them into office or of those wealthy entities who presently finance their campaigns? Were the hands of these special-interest lobbyists taken out of the asses of our politicians, then surely they'd care more for the opinion of their voters.

Besides the possibility of finding ways to publicly finance the campaigns of legitimate political candidates, the solution to this problem seems simple enough (at least from my uneducated standpoint). And that is to make it so that all donations are made anonymously and that there be a thousand dollar maximum. Anyone and their grandmother could make a donation, and the politicians won't have a clue who it's from. And even if they did, a grand hardly buys much favor these days.

Furthermore, politicians should no longer be allowed to accept lobbyist-funded junkets.

Not that this'll stop bribery altogether, mind you, but at the least it'd put an end to the legal bribery of such special-interest lobbying/campaign donations. Any money (or "gifts") knowingly given to a politician should be considered a flat-out bribe, whether used for their campaign or on themselves personally.

'Tis difficult to imagine any significant changes happening in our society until the way the government itself works is fixed, improved, reformed.

You can't get far in a broken car. Neither in a dysfunctional government. Our government seems to cause as many problems as it helps solve. If our society is like a giant heart, then our government is that heart's main and most clogged artery. It isn't reasonable to continue putting all our interest in what that artery can do us the entire heart until the blockage is cleared, lest we should only succeed at making the entire heart weaker and weaker.

Therefore the task our government should most intensely be concerning itself with right now is overhauling and improving its own state; how can the government improve the state of the country if its own state is less than functional?

I'm not suggesting the answer to all our problems lies within the government. To be sure, any real improvement made to the state of our nation will require the assistance of people on many different personal and social levels. But there's no denying our government is one of the greatest influences shaping our society; nor is there any denying the need to reverse the negative impact our government is currently having on much of our society.

But those on Capitol Hill won't make any such changes a reality without the massive support of their constituents. And so raises the question of what approach best influences the decisions of our political representatives.

It has been said that if you don't vote then you don't have the right to complain. I couldn't disagree more. Generally speaking, I'd assume that those who don't vote have even *more* of a reason to complain, since often the reason they didn't vote was because they felt there was no one worth voting for (which is usually true), and they'd rather choose no one than the less of two heels. 'Cause if our officials are reflective of those who elect them, then often the smartest thing one can do *is* not vote (sad as that may sound). This isn't to encourage people not to vote, but to demand more of our representatives.

Intelligence is something one must judge on a case by case, individual basis—mostly it takes a moderate amount of intelligence on the part of the judge to recognize this in others.

For some, though, it's easier just to look for this notion of what's "righteous," and anyone who mumbles this rhetoric like a broken record must make for a good politician, right? No. Wrong. A politician needs more than this glossy PR image of having "a strong moral base" to be effective in our government; it also takes a moderate amount of common sense, appreciation of logic, or just a basic grasp on reality, something too many politicians (especially those in the House and Senate) seem to be seriously lacking.

Why? Because voters judge candidates based on some shallow assessment of "character"; because voters, by and large, still like to be coddled by politicians like so many insecure babes. It's already a well established caricature that politicians are all truth-benders who'll tell the voting public whatever they must in order to get elected—yet that's still how voters continue to be wooed to one candidate over another, impressed by some vague rambling of how grand they'll make everything (somehow), never mind addressing the specific ills which plague our nation.

Only when voters begin to judge and scrutinize candidates on their actual knowledge and ideas will the quality of our politicians improve. We all must take the blame for the ineptitude of our own elected officials, and only we will be able to improve this.

Hopefully, with the spread of the personal computer and access to the Internet, the public will find more effective ways to take direct control over the government; to brush up on what's happening within the government and give our representatives a sincere piece of mind concerning it.

The real power of a republic such as ours isn't just in the right to vote. Voting by itself is such a little voice of what the people would like to see happen. No, the real power lies in the *promise* of a vote. We've all been told how constituency means we can influence the decisions of those we vote into office by sharing our opinions with them. So long as lobbyists and corporations control the campaign process for political candidates, then constituency won't mean jack.

But seeing as how the prospect of campaign reform has recently come to light, with a little (or a lot) more prodding, the House and Senate might indeed overhaul the manner in which their campaigns are financed. Once that happens the public is gonna have to be prepared to be the voice that most influences the decisions made by our representatives. We're gonna have to make sure the voice that shapes those decisions is an informed one, and that it's a voice that can instigate positive change.

UNTITLED

Our world, especially our own society, has seen some encouraging changes of late, not only in terms of industry and technology, but, even more impressively, in the general consciousness. Only recently have people broken with the rotted corpse of tradition towards more free-thinking, open-minded approaches to life.

Reactionary-types are now championing traditionalism as that to which we must return for guidance. Ralph Reed, formerly of the Christian Coalition (who—*big surprise*—traces the decline of the idealistic two-parent household to our country's social ills), believes America is at the start of a social movement which will take 40 to 50 years to reach fruition, and that in the end America will turn toward religious conservatives for leadership. He believes that voters long for a "moral renewal, a values renewal. That's the wave of the future." The Christian Coalition's revolutionary wave of the future is to have prayer in public classrooms—and who knows what else—and to illegalize abortion.

Has our culture actually so lost touch with its moral roots that people must backpedal to its oldest of institutions?

I don't know, but (taking this even further out-there) supposing I were an alien or some other hypothetical entity observing our planet and its many occupants from a heavenly perspective, specifically the comings and goings of us humans the most highly evolved species, I think I'd be fairly hopeful for our sorry-ass American asses. Because when you think about it, the rate at which we've mentally evolved in the past century is remarkable.

The civil rights movement and general rise in knowledge that's occurred recently and which is still underway—I'd think that this would be seen as a most wonderful sign of growth, especially taking into consideration our long history of barbarity. Considering that in its founding America represented what has always been wrong with humanity: the lack of it that allowed such things as the Crusades, the Inquisitions, and the Holocaust to occur, among endless other atrocities throughout history.

So to see us here in the United States—a people deeply rooted in this tradition with slavery, racism and sexism rampant throughout our entire mainstream society—evolve so strongly in consciousness would be encouraging indeed.

Yet the way these religious conservatives carry on, you'd think what's happened in the past century was *the* most detrimental thing to ever happen, and that the cause of our present problems is the fact that we *have* been moving away from their traditional, ideological, compartmentalized beliefs. They've deluded themselves into believing that the further back in time you go the stronger our moral base was, and that only *recently* has this faulted. When in fact the exact opposite is true in that only in the last half century has there arisen a truly civil consciousness.

It's easy to romanticize the past and ignore how the world's *always* been plagued with racism, sexism, and general inhumanity—it's pretty convenient to want to forget just how ignorant of this life we've always been. It's even easier to say that these problems now coming to the surface are a *result* of this movement away from the past, away from these familiar institutions.

This is certainly easier than it is to recognize that conservatism has been the norm for all history, and yet still these problems, these issues, and our own ignorance regarding them persisted. These traditional institutions have done little in progressing the knowledge of mankind. They've mostly acted as an anchor for people afraid of tread-

ing the unpredictable waters of life—afraid of drowning in the un-
charted depths of their own mind.

On a certain level these anchors of tradition help prevent people
from drifting back into more negative waters; but they also keep us
from moving forward or from making any positive progress. Well,
we've been sitting still long enough. The time has come to lift anchor,
hoist sail, and go exploring.

It's man's continuing dependence on the past—for a sense of identity
and direction—which holds us back, keeping millions in this country
and billions around the world fearfully reluctant to almost any kind of
real change. Humans have an innate fear of change, for we have an innate fear of the unknown, and change is often a dive straight into the
unknown. The unknown simply being everything we were born not
knowing—that which is therefore meant to be learned.

Humanity will never crawl from its ruts if the general population is
continually afraid of change; of allowing, contributing to, or initiating
change themselves. Seems most people would prefer to travel only
those passageways already carved out by our forebears, following always in their footsteps. People afraid to follow their own path in life;
afraid to realize their own creative powers.

Afraid to realize the power everybody has to change their reality.

Apprehension certainly is a component of intelligence, for only a
fool jumps into something blindly, and change is not good in and of itself as it can be either positive or negative. Yet, rather than go through
the laborious process of individual reason, most people have a tendency to use their fear and suspicion as a shortcut to judgment. And
people then stubbornly oppose change on the basis of this, their apprehension to anything new or unfamiliar.

I look around our world and it's like fingernails desperately and
persistently clawing onto the past, digging our nails deeply into it, refusing to accept time, refusing to evolve. It's as if our world is being
haunted by memories—the past is haunting us into our graves. The
past is dead, let it rest so that we may *live*. The only place of life is now.
Right here and right now. We must recognize the past for what it is and

realize that we've been growing out of and away from this state of ignorance and egotism.

It's unnecessary for the psyche of mankind to have deep roots in the
past, like trees practically. It sounds funny, but in a strange meta-
phorical sense mankind does have a plant-like mentality, except man
plants its roots in the dead soil that is the past. But it's unnatural for
our mindsets to be so dependent on preconceived notions of absolute
truth. This sets boundaries on us mentally like trees are limited
physically, compartmentalized into a specifically narrow awareness.

It's time for us to carve out our own understanding, our own knowledge of the world in which we live, the lives we lead, which are our own
and not dependent on these remnants of old.

I'm not saying the past should be forgotten; by all means no. It has
much to teach us, and the basis for much of our modern knowledge
originated in the past, so the prospect of forgetting the past is unthink-
able. That does not mean, however, that we must be *enslaved* by the
past, oppressed or limited only to that which is already established.
We must use the past for the invaluable service it provides, using what
knowledge it can teach us as a stepping stone toward progression, toward learning more and more about ourselves, toward constantly improving the condition of our lives.

Step up on the ladder that is the past while letting go of it; entertain
notions of the future, especially immediate; but mostly live in and for
the present, day by day, moment to moment.

According to Webster's dictionary, conservative means: "Tending to
preserve established traditions or institutions and to resist or oppose
any changes in these." Change is essential to all living things; it's what
most distinguishes us from *non-living* things. Change is essential not
only because our society is troubled, but because everything should
be open to change. There will never be a perfect belief system, government, or society that can forever be set in stone. Life must remain
fluid in order for us to constantly evolve.

Don't get me wrong, I'm not advocating change for its own sake either; certainly not. Webster's definition for "liberal" is almost nothing

but positive—people still get carried away with this notion, though, endorsing change on an ideological basis over reason or moderation. Extremism truly goes all ways. The most important thing is not to approach these issues and questions of life from any biased perspective (like that associated with silly labels like liberal and conservative, Democrat and Republican)—it is only from our own individual perspective that anyone will be able to envision a unique or plausible approach to this crazy life. We must confront these issues from the bottom up, start from scratch and see what original visions we can be inspired to create. But if we approach it always from the pre-formed perspective of our peers, our state, or of our religious leaders, then we're doomed to endlessly repeat what's already been tried without ever progressing past that point.

For all the progress that's been made recently, it will more than likely pale in comparison to the transcendence in awareness that is ripe to happen in the near future and soon-to-be-present, what you and I and everyone alive today will play a very direct role in the outcome of.

Never before has our present-day lives and the future before us been so much in the hands of all individual beings as opposed to based in stone-like ideologies, institutions and religions. Our lives, our future, is totally in our own hands.

Can you feel the excitement?

Even today, with my newfound passion and conviction for all that happens in our world, I still find myself hesitant to believe that anything I do, write or say will make any difference whatsoever. The major difference between then and now is that I no longer allow my fear of failure or my cynicism to act as a barrier to caring; to making some sort of effort to contribute something positive, knowing all too well it may not add up to squat in the end.

There are no guarantees in this world—you just have to do the best you can in the hope things eventually turn out for the better. No, your contribution may not mean a goddamned thing when all this is over, but so what? One who loves themselves is obliged to participate in this struggle simply out of their subsequent love for humanity. Those who become involved do so for themselves, because they care about and love themselves and then extend this love to the world they inhabit. Whether the action actually makes a significant impact is inconsequential to the value of the act in and of itself. An act of goodness and love is its own reward, and doubts as to whether or not it makes a difference shouldn't prevent someone from becoming involved, from taking some sort of initiative to make this screwed-up, upside-down world of ours a nicer place.

Yeah, that's right, my parents were hippies . . . you wanna make something of it, punkass?

FINAL THOUGHT:

WHO FRICKIN' CARES IF RUSH LIMBAUGH IS WRONG!?

Alright, so Rush Limbaugh is wrong. Unequivocally, indisputably, just-plain-wrong. But is this even a topic that needed clarification? Hardly. When elaborated on, though, Limbaugh represented something which allowed me to discuss any number of related issues. I doubt you could have gotten this far without noticing how my book isn't even really *about* Limbaugh, not entirely, and how this is a *good* thing (at least in moi's opinion).

If you flipped to the last chapter hoping to find a neat summary or conclusion as to why Limbaugh is wrong, you'll be disappointed. (Hell, most of my major conclusions can be found in the first chapter.) I could give you some elaborate theory about how Limbaugh is simply looking to assure himself that life isn't any more complex than the comforting picture of simplicity that is conservatism; or that the reason he blames everything on liberals is because his delusions of order requires an enemy against which to proclaim his own sense of victory; or how he conveniently sidesteps any intelligent debate on the issues by characterizing his opposition only by the most fringe of extremists.

I *could* tell you these things, but why bother? Most of these conclusions are self-evident. And besides, that's not why I wrote this.

Other than presenting a few thoughts on how our society might be improved, my underlying intention was to somehow inspire people. My hope was that this book would fill people with a longing to expand on what I've written, so that it acts mainly as a catalyst for something real in the real world, rather than just a lot of overly contrived words on these pieces of paper.

Am I a dreamer or what?

PRIDE AND REGRET

The thing I'm probably *proudest* of this book is that I edited it by myself and kept my voice intact, which I fear would have been diluted into some impersonal fact-sheet had this landed into the hands of a major publisher. At least that's the impression I got from the feedback given to me concerning my book proposal.

I despised having to write a query letter, trying to sell my book via what could only by definition be in crass and commercial terms. The queries I sent out were usually pretty crummy; but I expected people to be impressed with my ideas, not the slickness of my query letter. Most of the rejections I got were anonymous form-letters. But some of the more elaborate explanations I got were real hoots. One person wrote simply that, "At least Limbaugh is literate." But the most riotous letter I received is that in Appendix VIII.

As you might imagine the letter I wrote back was less than grateful. I don't know, maybe this person is right, maybe what I've written here is more suited for Letters to the Editor than an actual book. But what I can't get over are statements like, "Do you know the powerful machine backing him?" and, "What is more important to an editor is what have you found out about the group backing him, etc." and, "What is behind his propaganda?" My God man, the way this guy talks you'd think all professional book editors were a bunch of conspiracy theorists who believe there's some underground agency that funds R.L.'s shows. When obviously the only reason he had a television show, much like the same reason he has a radio show, is because there's an audience who wants to listen to him. The free marketplace is the only force backing Limbaugh's success. As for what spurns his conservative views, that is the playground of speculation and very much a matter of personal opinion.

My indignant pride aside, it seems only fitting that I also end this with an acknowledgment of the book's very weaknesses, of which it contains more than its share. The greatest of which probably being a lack of confirmation of facts; I didn't do a fraction as much research as I could have to confirm or elaborate on many things of which I wrote. But I made a conscious decision from the get-go that I'd rather write something of interest on its own subjective merit, and the last thing I wanted to do was clutter my words up with a lot of boring facts. (Well, that and I'm real lazy.)

What I do feel regret for is the fact that I've accused Limbaugh of making broad generalizations against liberals, while at the same I've done practically the same thing towards conservatives. I am likewise guilty of using the term conservative in an overreaching and derogatory context. I fully appreciate that religious conservatives are individuals who, like everyone else, hold their own personal opinions and viewpoints, and I'd like to sincerely apologize to anyone whom I might have insulted or unfairly characterized.

ONE LAST RANT, THEN I'M OUTTAHERE

It's just that, often, many of "conservative" creed seem too easily agreeable with popular opinion, too willing to conform to conventional standards, a little too eager to simply go along with wherever their leaders (such as Limbaugh's tide) may take them. Limbaugh, his listeners, and countless others around the world earnestly believe that through their brand of conservative ideology and religious mythology they have the perfect little truth and simplistic answer to everything. That's what an ideology does—it oversimplifies everything, takes life and reduces it to the crudest of concepts.

This is the sad legacy of our cerebrally-challenged kind.

But I say no longer. It's time to educate ourselves about that which eludes us; to confront our fears; and to delve into and embrace the mysteries of life so many faiths conveniently insist are beyond human understanding.

Not to deny that humans need some form of outside guidance in life (other than one's parents, needless to say). In a "Mythology" course I once took, we read many cultures mythologies dating from time back when, and whereas most were pretty twisted, a few struck me as uniquely uplifting. The Native American mythologies concerning their relationship with the Earth, for instance, struck me as being very wise, for I myself feel a strong connection and love for the natural world. Thereafter I began to realize that having a "mythology" (or spiritual philosophy, as it were) is essential to mankind. Essential in helping us understand ourselves and this life; essential in helping guide us for natural self-guidance eludes us.

But guide us toward what?

Individuality, self-guidance of course. Towards that which eludes us, away from the very ignorance that makes us need these mythologies and religions to begin with.

The most positive philosophy I can envision would be that which helps guide one *away* from that philosophy, that wants to be abandoned or transcended in favor of self-guidance and self-truth. That wants to guide people to a place so that it is no longer even necessary, away from itself. Not a mythology, philosophy or religious ideology that feeds off of and exploits people's ignorance and fear, making them increasingly dependent on it for guidance like the mental, emotional, spiritual crutch it so often is.

That's all I'm saying and the reason I wrote this book. Not to pick on Limbaugh, necessarily, but simply to express something different, another outlook. To encourage people to open their eyes, their minds, and their hearts a little. To look through the illusion of objective, preconceived truth personified by past and modern-day ideologies. And to perhaps take a more realistic look at how things in our society and world might be changed for the better.

But please, don't take my word for anything. For above all else, my real wish (other than that Limbaugh doesn't *sue* my ass into the poorhouse) is that people search for their own answers, their own truths, their own paths of guidance in life.

That's it ...

That's why Rush Limbaugh is wrong.

APPENDIXES

The first draft of this book was just short of 300 pages and loaded with slumberous deadwood. It was only through labor intensive editing and rewriting that I was able to streamline this into what you now hold in your hands. I'd still have preferred it to be at least 200 pages, though: at 135 pages, suddenly my epic is looking more like the pamphlet I spoke of in the prelude than a real book. I'm definitely suffering from spine envy. I know size isn't supposed to matter and all that, but still, I'm feeling just a *little* inadequate here. And so I admit with faint trepidation that these appendixes were born mainly of my desire to put a bit more meat on these skinny bones.

Everything here is something I'm proud of, but, for different reasons, also stuff I considered deleting. Appendix I, for instance, was originally the first chapter after the prelude. But, fond as I am of the piece, I felt it was a bad way to open the book, and would only have succeeded in alienating all those whose musical tastes may differ radically from my own.

The rest of the appendixes, however, are (by and large) just so much more misplaced padding.

RUSH TO JUDGMENT

He called Kurt Cobain human trash. Who in the *fuck* is this over-bloated sack of protoplasm to pass judgment on Kurt Cobain?

Cobain was an incredibly talented musician, as is the rest of Nirvana, who, it could be said in no uncertain terms, had more than his share of personal demons, dabbled heavily in heroin and tried committing suicide a couple times. He was an intense, passionate young man (all of which poured through his music), and, whereas I didn't idolize the guy in the least, I had a great deal of respect and admiration for Kurt Cobain.

It was April 11th, '94, and after flipping between crappy reruns of *MASH* and *Late Show with David Letterman*, I tuned over to Rush Limbaugh 'cause, in his own warped way, he's fairly amusing. Like a good car accident. Or the Hindenburg. I rarely ever watched his show, though, but at the time I got a total of three channels through some rinky-dink bunny-ear antenna on top my TV and my only selections opposite him were *A Current Affair* and *Nightline*, so I was always jumping back and forth between them.

Well, before taking a sponsor break from his effervescent flow of wisdom, Limbaugh said that when they returned he wanted to talk about Kurt Cobain who had shot himself with a shotgun. What?! Could it be true? *Had he killed himself?*

Kurt's corpse was discovered on a Friday; I learned of his death on Limbaugh's Monday broadcast. Somehow I'd heard nothing about it; although over the weekend a local radio station had had some special on Nirvana, and in-between songs they played clips of other musicians talking about how much pressure there was in that kind of life. I didn't make anything of it at the time—except to enjoy the music—but now, thinking back, it must've been a farewell tribute.

Limbaugh wanted to talk about how the media was hyping Cobain as the voice of my generation—I'm nineteen, is that my generation? And Rush had a valid point, the media undeniably was blowing Kurt's image, basically the image they created for him, way out of proportion—the "voice" of a generation, give me a break! A hell of a musician?, sure, but the "spokesman for a generation"? Kurt Cobain was no more the voice of my generation than Rush Limbaugh is the lone voice of conservatism, as I'm sure there are many conservatives who don't feel Rush represents their views (entirely).

But to make this point, Limbaugh sacrificed Cobain on his self-righteous cross. He called him human trash (or, to be perfectly precise, his exact words were "worthless shred of human debris"), and said he looked filthy and rotten and that if he did clean himself up his audience would go away, which is utter nonsense. The only reason Nirvana sold millions of records and are as popular as they are, or were, is because their music is genuinely good (in my *subjective* opinion—you simply cannot be objective about music, what's good or not and what kind of person this makes you . . . that is, apparently, unless you're Rush Limbaugh).

If Nirvana's not to your particular taste, fine, that's fine. There's lots of music I don't especially care for. And, if I wanted, I'm sure I could find stuff to trash about, say, country singers . . . if I searched in the most shallow depths of my mind, sure, I could probably get carried away too. But I try not to let such sorry thoughts get the better of me, although I am fully aware of them, thus recognizing the stupidity of the thoughts and not dwelling, mesmerizing, and obsessing over them like Limbaugh seems to do. I discard such thoughts because I know they're below petty—I don't know *what* Rush thinks about?!

Why couldn't Limbaugh just say the media was blowing his image out of proportion and leave it at that? Why'd he have to assassinate Cobain's character as well?

Course now that I've had prolonged (and way painful) exposure to Limbaugh, in retrospect the attack shouldn't have been unexpected. The fact is he's always doing this kind of shit—always crucifying people's characters just to make some insignificant point, usually about how lacking in character everyone is but himself and the fans who cheer him on. (Limbaugh's flattering condolence on the occasion of Jerry Garcia's death was: "When you strip it all away, Jerry Garcia destroyed his life on drugs. And yet he's being honored, like some godlike figure. Our priorities are out of whack, folks.")

Yes, the media blew Cobain's image *way* out of proportion; and no, Nirvana didn't break the mold either. But why can't I be allowed to personally appreciate something without me or that thing being attacked by self-righteous morality police?

To answer my own question of why Limbaugh did this, it's clear his motivation went well beyond simple annoyance of all the attention Kurt's suicide received. For starters, Limbaugh isn't able to look past the circumstances surrounding someone's death and observe the content of their life, and even were he able to do so he'd probably still judge Cobain's (or Garcia's) life by his mostly superficial standards.

Secondly, though, is the fact that Limbaugh believes kids who listen to Nirvana and music of the like have given up on America and the American dream. He said at the end of his Cobain crucifixion that our country hasn't run out of opportunities, we're in spiffy shape, and that the new rebellion among young people today is becoming *conservative* (a good laugh).

Having been submersed in the media coverage surrounding Cobain's suicide, the most common theme I found was this exhausted portrayal of today's youth as a bunch of sardonic slackers with no ambition to do anything with their useless lives. And of Kurt Cobain being called an "angry young man" (the media obviously has a difficult time distinguishing passion from anger—not that I'm any expert on the subject myself, but, still . . .).

However, I'll most happily grant that much of today's youth is pretty lost and just way out there somewhere. But this has nada to do with Kurt Cobain, Nirvana, or "grunge." Certain not-to-be-named people in the media (which is just my slick way of saying I couldn't remember who they were even if I wanted to) made it sound as though this attitude of the crowd most often associated with youth-orientated grunge/punk/hard-rock was just part of the *fad*—a fad that Nirvana helped to create, no less!

The fucking media, I swear. Talk about condescending!

To suggest, as some of these post-Cobain-suicide articles have, that Nirvana and such new bands helped to create this "grunge" sensation of teen angst is to be ignorant of history, of what it's like being a teenager period (especially in this day and age). "Grunge" was created *around* bands like Nirvana by the pop-culture media that's always looking for a new fad to exploit and cash in on. Teenage angst has always been and always will; the rages of youth have nothing to do with Nirvana or "grunge"—these things simply helped magnify it for those who'd never have noticed or cared otherwise.

To begin with, Limbaugh and other critics who have such a painfully difficult time understanding these youths must realize that their cynicism isn't economic so much as it is cultural. Sure, the chance to excel and become financially successful still exists for today's youth, but what kind of country do they want to live in in the meantime?

What choice do they have?

Our society isn't measured by the strength of its economy by those of us (particularly the young) who haven't yet been numbed into these monetary-worshipping robots enough to blindly ignore the fuckedup-ness of our society, of our world. This isn't to deny the importance of the economy to any society, but ultimately the economy is secondary in significance to the *culture* of the society it supports. It is *not* the society, however, and a country can have a strong economy (like ours) and still be perfectly screwed.

Today's society is so radically different than it's ever been, than it was not twenty years ago! AIDS can kill you just by having sex, inner city gang violence has spread out like a cancer to all regions of our nation, and the gangsta image has become a popular trend everywhere. The crime rate may be fairly steady, but homicide among 10 to 17 year olds has jumped upwards of 100% in the past decade. Violence is out of control; hostility and paranoia rule the streets in parts of the country. Fear is palpable. Our government's a corrupt, bureaucratic mess that most of the time seems beyond comprehension. The world is at its most vulnerable ever, what with nuclear power, environmental abuse, and the ominous threat of WW3.

And whereas the norm heretofore has always been "authority figures" telling our society to think like this, act like that, believe in this (or else), our youth has finally begun to ask, "Or else *what*?" Today's kids have grown up in a society so screwed-up and frightening that many have begun to think for *themselves,* to question everything, to seek their *own* answers and *own* truths.

The very idea of true individuality, though said to have been the passion of this country's founders, is not readily accepted or even understood. Our society still very-much-so encourages conformity, as has been the case of pretty much all known civilizations. Conformity through ideology—and mythology—based on written documents, words that are supposed to shape our souls, our conscious, our emotions and feelings; guide our actions, dictate our lives.

So when I hear the media droning about the emergence of a strong subculture that has become disenchanted with our society, I have to tell you the honest truth: this strikes me as absolutely wonderful! Now this truly gives me hope. Why does the mainstream assume that being "disillusioned" with society is a bad thing, anyway? I mean, think about the word for a moment. I'd think being able to see through an illusion would be a *good* thing. "Illusionment" is the bad thing, that which most in our society and world suffer from. (But of course wouldn't you know it, there's no such word as "illusionment"—then how'd they come up with *"dis*illusionment"?!)

It's the society and its largest and most powerful institutions that harbor such illusions, that encourages everyone to adhere to such. Why? To insure security and stability, for it is generally perceived that people are not ready to accept reality—such as the reality of the individual power, control and responsibility each of us possess over our own lives, our own thoughts and actions.

Yes, much of our youth is pretty directionless, and no, this does not automatically mean that they *are* going to find their own will or realize their own individuality; this does not promise a better future simply by virtue of their disenchantment. Truth is still something they must realize on their own, as does everyone, but freeing your mind from the shackles of too many ignorantly preconceived false ideas, ideologies and mythologies of life in the universe, is as good a beginning place toward this as anything.

Freeing your mind and opening yourself up to the possibility of *personal* truth.

Considering it in relative perspective to the rest of humankind's history, I think that right now we have the best possible chance we've ever had for genuinely positive change. On the same token, we have the greatest possible chance ever of totally fucking ourselves, our society, and our planet up to all hell.

Enjoy the ride.

— a sort of farewell tribute of my own —

Over these past—and last—few tumultuous years of my latter teens, I've listened almost exclusively to classical music and classic rock. But in my early teens (decades ago, it seems) I listened to and loved with a passion punk.

For myself, at least, it began with the Sex Pistols, then on to such great and memorable bands as Minor Threat, The Adolescents, The Descendants, Suicidal Tendencies, what else?—a few other bands. Punk rock—to me—was this rejection of conformity and authority and everything mundane. The music was there to express all the fucked-up, conflicting things I was feeling, to scream it all out for me, to act as some sort of catharsis and give me some kind of voice.

And Nirvana's like what the potential for much of the punk I listened to could've been, come true, and it's fucking beautiful! (For some reason the word "grunge" grates on me as though I were a hunk o' cheese, and I refuse to use it except in condescension.)

I've never possessed any musical talent of my own, yet for as long as memory serves I've yearned for the ability to create such sweet sounds.

Christ man, I wish I could sing like that; I wish I could write and create and play music like that. I have a weak singing voice to begin with, yet I can sing along with a few bands and Elvis Presley's easy to exaggerate. But I can't even come close to what Cobain could do with his voice. It was a raw and blistering thing—not defined or polished, yet no less spectacular in its modest range and intoxicating intensity. It wasn't *what* he had so much as *how* he used it; he sang much like his music sounded, almost always teetering on, playing with, or otherwise stretching the limits of the straining level.

And his lyrics were so, I don't know, I hate to even dare risk sounding pretentious—too late—but they were almost kinda profound at times (or perhaps really, really *neat* is better descriptive). They didn't always make perfect sense, and, no Rush, you can't always understand what he's singing, but so what? Music is emotional; it doesn't *have* to tell a story or have a moral for sound's sake!

All I know is that, at the time, the music he and his band created was more passionate and inspiring than anything I'd heard in a long time.

Then he done went and killed himself. And I didn't even know the fucking guy and yet still I felt genuinely bad when I learned of his death, for selfish reasons no less: 'cause I liked his music. Yet in a way it was more than that—there was just something there, in him and in his music, that I felt a strange almost-kinship to.

It's peculiar that I'd be haunted by thoughts of someone I never even met. Perhaps because I'd only just started listening to Nirvana a few weeks before his death. Or because I was feeling especially estranged at the time and wanted someone to identify with. For whatever reason, the thought of all that might have been had he lived on gnawed away at me for a good time after his death. He was just 27 and in his prime. Full of possibilities. There one second, then the next just . . . gone. Like a glorious flame burning bright with illumination suddenly snuffed out by an unseen gust—just phssst! And all that's left is the music, simultaneously beautiful and, for a time, haunting of all that might have but was never to be.

Perhaps calling yourself a liberal actually meant something at one time. But because it's been typified by those who take progressivism to the furthest extreme, to characterize anyone Limbaugh disagrees with, the word's lost all meaning (at least in my mind). It's probably for the best, too. Who wants to limit themselves, the range of their mind and consciousness, to the confines of any ideological label?

I consider myself neither liberal or conservative.

Nor am I a Democrat or a Republican; those words mean nothing to me. I am first and foremost an individual. And I'm not afraid of coming to my own conclusions, of seeking my own answers. I only hope others will also step forward into a greater understanding of themselves and this world, where they do not derive their sense of self, truth, or guidance from other people's preconceived classifications and ideologies.

Make no mistake that many Democrats are as guilty of mean-spirited partisanship as their Republican counterparts. While playing that Fleetwood Mac song *Don't Stop* ("don't stop thinking about to-morrow/it'll be better than before"), Clinton paid no heed to the final passage in the song: "Don't you look back." He, along with other Democrats, have rather pathetically obsessed over the corruption allegations leveled towards the Reagan/Bush administration to contrast their own idealism *way* too much. (Although in light of all the allegations leveled at his own administration, it's unlikely Clinton will continue to be as eager to point out the faults of those he's succeeding.) And it just generally seems that for every Republican politician spouting rhetoric about the evil Democrats, there's an equal amount of Democrats spouting the same crap about the evil Republicans.

Choosing a political party in America is like choosing sides on opposing football teams. In the end partisanship is a frivolous sport, where any yardage gained by one team, or rather party, amounts to little more than a lot of back-patting and ballyhooing. It's only natural that people be divided in their beliefs, but this doesn't mean people must be divided *because* of their beliefs. I look forward to the day when we transcend the categorized labels and the name-blaming, where an idea is just an idea expressed by an individual valued for its own merit.

SHHH!
IS SILENCE A PRAYER?

On the specific subject of classroom prayer again, though I wouldn't necessarily *encourage* this, but for those schools that decide they want it I see nothing terribly objectionable to a daily moment of silence being held in public classrooms.

Some rather reactionary school board members have spoken out against this as a connection between church and state. According to The Outlook of Santa Monica, CA, Lillian Raffel, president of the Beverly Hills school board, said of this: "It's an implied prayer. It really is. I just think it's treading on dangerous ground, when you have a routine moment of silence. I think that people interpret [prayer] as the intent." Another member of the B.H. school board named A.J. Wilmer said of it: ". . . I think people are advocating it for religious reasons. In fact, they see a moment of silence as a nice way to say prayer in school."

Yeah, so? If they want, those of strong religious faith can and most probably will designate the time to say a silent little prayer to themselves (and it can apply to and not infringe on anyone's religion). But it can also be a non-religious moment for anyone else, whether cynic or atheist or someone who just doesn't know what they yet believe. Some may just enjoy the silence, accept it as an opportunity to reflect on their life, on their classes, with a little perspective. A moment to just soak it all in. Others may simply fiddle their thumbs, doodle on their notebooks, or pass notes to one another. My point being, no matter what any student chooses to do with that time, it's totally their own, infringing only on their right to make noise, which is all they do the rest of the day anyway.

Sometimes a moment of silence can make all the noise just that much clearer.

I honestly don't understand how any sensible person could interpret this as anything but the most harmless of activities whose sole purpose is to address the emotional chaos of most individuals in this life, especially a young person in school. (Some people have promoted a moment of silence to help "build character" and turn students into "good citizens": I think that's a lot o' crap! But of all the things schools *do* force onto their students—including "guidance" counseling—what could possibly be more passive or harmless than a moment of silence?) In fact in some cases I believe it'd be a very reasonable compromise for those schools with a large religious student body.

MEDICINAL MARY

The medical applications of marijuana are rather considerable. Not that this has stopped our government from forbidding its medical use: only eight people are legally allowed to smoke marijuana under the Compassionate Use Investigational New Drug program. The procedure to enlist on this program was an estimated 50 hours of paperwork; although once Bob Randall (the man for whom the program was originated so that he could legally smoke marijuana to treat his glaucoma, thus preventing him from going *blind*) developed a quicker way of applying, applications soared, and so the George Bush administration mercilessly killed the program in 1992 ("gotta look *tough on crime*, Mr. President").

Legal medical use of marijuana is more strictly prohibited than drugs such as morphine, codeine and cocaine. Justifying this tight-fisted control over the medical use of marijuana, Rayford Kytle, a spokesman for the Public Health Service (which oversees the FDA), said, "We . . . are concerned that we send out a consistent message on drugs, that they are not healthy and they are not good, especially for young people." Yeah, the last thing they want to do is come anywhere near admitting the truth, especially if it can benefit the health of people with AIDS, cancer and other illnesses.

A DRUGGIE SMOKED MY HOMEWORK

As for Limbaugh, you'd think someone so concerned for the jobs of tobacco-pickers would be equally enthusiastic about the many jobs hemp legalization would produce. The industrial benefits of the hemp fabric, which is derived from the marijuana stem, is many. Hemp is an amazingly versatile fabric that can be used to make any number of quality products. One acre of hemp can make as much paper as four acres of forest. The original drafts of the Declaration of Independence were written on hemp paper, as were the sails of many pioneers ships made from hemp cloth. George Washington, Thomas Jefferson, and Abraham Lincoln were all huge proponents of hemp because they knew what an amazing plant cannabis is and of all its possible uses, industrial and . . . personal?

I don't know how many of you saw the movie *Dazed and Confused*, but in it was a scene in which this one pothead talks about what a major stoner Washington was. In context of the movie it sounded like a lot of rambling b.s., and I don't know whether there was a grain of truth to any of it. But in the contexts of pure speculation, seeing as how they were such champions of hemp, is it not then within the realm of possibility that tobacco wasn't the only thing those old timers were sticking in their pipes?

Heck if I know!? There's no denying, though, that our history books have always been somewhat selective in what information they chose to disclose . . . or distort.

WORKIN' FOR THA MAN

And instead of just watching TV all day, inmates should be encouraged to participate in productive activities from wit to better themselves. Including working to make products (like that prison in Oregon that makes the Prison Blues clothes), the profits from which could help finance their own imprisonment. Since they'd be doing skilled tasks a bit more precise than breaking rocks, the convicts would have to work of their own choice, which means paying them minimum wage.

On a purely superficial level, what's the problem with most criminals? They don't have a job, man! They lazy, irresponsible. It's fair to assume many crimes are economically motivated. So why not teach them a skill they can use in the real world once paroled, teach them a work ethic? Many of these people have never held a steady job—they may find they like working for their money (they should get around 15-20% of their salaries, the rest going to support their own cost in a prison and to a Victim Fund organization).

Course careful consideration would have to be made as to how any and all prison-made products might effect American businesses. Nobody would want to see law-abiding citizens losing their jobs to law-breaking prisoners. The Prison Blues Clothes, for instance, sell successfully (especially in Asia for some reason), yet hardly makes a dent in the multi-billion dollar jeans and clothing industry. But beyond that point, when they feel they might hurt American businesses, the prisons could turn to making products which aren't largely produced here because they're made in countries with such cheap labor we haven't been able to compete—but the prisons could easily compete with their cheap inmate labor.

If of good quality, I'm sure there are many Americans who'd be more than willing to buy prison-made products. For one, simply for the product itself, but also because they'd know they were helping to support the justice system, and the rehabilitation of the prisoners. No doubt people would be glad to support this system with the purchase of an actual product they wanted and chose, as opposed to just forking over their tax dollars.

ARBITRARY OBSERVATION:
¿NEGATIVE + NEGATIVE = POSITIVE?

Certain conservatives appear to believe that the best manner of encouragement is by discouraging the opposite. Rather than positively encourage birth, they negatively discourage abortion. Rather than encourage individuals to behave well by addressing them on the complicated soul, teaching them self-awareness and self-guidance, they do this by discouraging evil ways, and by inflicting those who *have* behaved badly to hellish punishment. Rather than try to end illegitimacy by going after the abandoners, they try to end single motherhood by stigmatizing the abandoned and scorning Murphy Brown. And rather than encourage the homeless to pick themselves up for themselves, they say this must be done to appease our disapproving society.

It's an unusual approach to life, to say the least. Many traditionalists I've observed seem to believe in guiding, or *forcing*, people towards a positive by discouraging the negative with a negative. I suppose in some ways it can almost be seen as a form of reverse-psychology, though I envision it more as being this magnetic theory wherein they believe that two negatives will force one toward the positive. Weird. Uh—heh—whatever.

Dear Michael Rahman: April 3, 1995

Thank you for your letter.

Anyone with any sense knows Rush Limbaugh is wrong. There are probably many professional writers preparing books and articles about that. Have you read all the articles already in print? Do you know of books being written? Why would a publisher put an unknown writer under contract for such a book when to an editor it would be obvious you are expressing your personal opinion rather than having done research inasmuch as you don't even look in a dictionary to see how "rebuttal" is spelled.

Instead of a book, opinions on subjects are better sent to Letters to the Editor. Do you know WHY R.L. is on television? Do you know the powerful machine backing him? Have you done any research? Or is your book just a reason for putting your own opinions in print?

Your outline is not organized correctly for your book. It doesn't matter what prompted you to write it. And it is not important how you first became aware of R.L. What is more important to an editor is what have you found out concerning the group backing him, etc.

You don't prove R.L. wrong by voicing your own ideas about the subjects he speaks about. What is behind his propaganda? That is the question.

I have a critique service you may want to use to come to grips with your book. The fee is $200. per 50,000 words, refundable when the book sells. If interested, send me the complete manuscript with fee and return postage.

Sincerely,
XXXXXX XXXXXXXXX

ACKNOWLEDGMENTS

I must extend my utmost gratitude to my mom, my stepdad, and the rest of my family for taking me in and supporting me while I did practically nothing but work on the completion of this oddity, and without whose generosity it might never have been published. Muchos gracias y'all.

ORDER FORM

WHY RUSH LIMBAUGH IS WRONG OR: THE DEMISE OF TRADI-
TIONALISM AND THE RISE OF PROGRESSIVE SENSIBILITY

Price: $16.00
Price for each additional book ordered: $12.00

Shipping:
$4.00 for first book and $2.00 for each additional book.

Sales Tax:
California residents please add 8.25%

Credit Card Orders: Call Toll Free: 1-800-431-1579
Have your AMEX, VISA, Discover, or MasterCard ready.
Make check or money order payable to **Mighty Pen Publishing.**
Send to:

> Mighty Pen Publishing
> 1223 Wilshire Blvd. #324
> Santa Monica, CA 90403

Name: _____

Address: _____

City: _____State: _____Zip:_____

ORDER FORM

WHY RUSH LIMBAUGH IS WRONG OR: THE DEMISE OF TRADI-
TIONALISM AND THE RISE OF PROGRESSIVE SENSIBILITY

Price: $16.00
Price for each additional book ordered: $12.00

Shipping:
$4.00 for first book and $2.00 for each additional book.

Sales Tax:
California residents please add 8.25%

Credit Card Orders: Call Toll Free: 1-800-431-1579
Have your AMEX, VISA, Discover, or MasterCard ready.
Make check or money order payable to **Mighty Pen Publishing.**
Send to:

> Mighty Pen Publishing
> 1223 Wilshire Blvd. #324
> Santa Monica, CA 90403

Name: _____

Address: _____

City: _____ State: _____ Zip: _____